C-4587   CAREER EXAMINATION SERIES

This is your
PASSBOOK for...

Project Manager I/II

Test Preparation Study Guide
Questions & Answers

COPYRIGHT NOTICE

This book is SOLELY intended for, is sold ONLY to, and its use is RESTRICTED to individual, bona fide applicants or candidates who qualify by virtue of having seriously filed applications for appropriate license, certificate, professional and/or promotional advancement, higher school matriculation, scholarship, or other legitimate requirements of education and/or governmental authorities.

This book is NOT intended for use, class instruction, tutoring, training, duplication, copying, reprinting, excerption, or adaptation, etc., by:

1) Other publishers
2) Proprietors and/or Instructors of "Coaching" and/or Preparatory Courses
3) Personnel and/or Training Divisions of commercial, industrial, and governmental organizations
4) Schools, colleges, or universities and/or their departments and staffs, including teachers and other personnel
5) Testing Agencies or Bureaus
6) Study groups which seek by the purchase of a single volume to copy and/or duplicate and/or adapt this material for use by the group as a whole without having purchased individual volumes for each of the members of the group
7) Et al.

Such persons would be in violation of appropriate Federal and State statutes.

PROVISION OF LICENSING AGREEMENTS – Recognized educational, commercial, industrial, and governmental institutions and organizations, and others legitimately engaged in educational pursuits, including training, testing, and measurement activities, may address request for a licensing agreement to the copyright owners, who will determine whether, and under what conditions, including fees and charges, the materials in this book may be used them. In other words, a licensing facility exists for the legitimate use of the material in this book on other than an individual basis. However, it is asseverated and affirmed here that the material in this book CANNOT be used without the receipt of the express permission of such a licensing agreement from the Publishers. Inquiries re licensing should be addressed to the company, attention rights and permissions department.

All rights reserved, including the right of reproduction in whole or in part, in any form or by any means, electronic or mechanical, including photocopying, recording, or by any information storage and retrieval system, without permission in writing from the Publisher.

Copyright © 2025 by
National Learning Corporation

212 Michael Drive, Syosset, NY 11791
(516) 921-8888 • www.passbooks.com
E-mail: info@passbooks.com

PASSBOOK® SERIES

THE *PASSBOOK® SERIES* has been created to prepare applicants and candidates for the ultimate academic battlefield – the examination room.

At some time in our lives, each and every one of us may be required to take an examination – for validation, matriculation, admission, qualification, registration, certification, or licensure.

Based on the assumption that every applicant or candidate has met the basic formal educational standards, has taken the required number of courses, and read the necessary texts, the *PASSBOOK® SERIES* furnishes the one special preparation which may assure passing with confidence, instead of failing with insecurity. Examination questions – together with answers – are furnished as the basic vehicle for study so that the mysteries of the examination and its compounding difficulties may be eliminated or diminished by a sure method.

This book is meant to help you pass your examination provided that you qualify and are serious in your objective.

The entire field is reviewed through the huge store of content information which is succinctly presented through a provocative and challenging approach – the question-and-answer method.

A climate of success is established by furnishing the correct answers at the end of each test.

You soon learn to recognize types of questions, forms of questions, and patterns of questioning. You may even begin to anticipate expected outcomes.

You perceive that many questions are repeated or adapted so that you can gain acute insights, which may enable you to score many sure points.

You learn how to confront new questions, or types of questions, and to attack them confidently and work out the correct answers.

You note objectives and emphases, and recognize pitfalls and dangers, so that you may make positive educational adjustments.

Moreover, you are kept fully informed in relation to new concepts, methods, practices, and directions in the field.

You discover that you are actually taking the examination all the time: you are preparing for the examination by "taking" an examination, not by reading extraneous and/or supererogatory textbooks.

In short, this PASSBOOK®, used directedly, should be an important factor in helping you to pass your test.

PROJECT MANAGER I/II

DUTIES

Project Managers apply a wide range of specialized knowledge, skills, tools, and techniques to direct and coordinate human and material resources at all phases of a project which includes origination, initiation, planning, execution and control, and closeout. A project is a temporary effort with defined objectives and results undertaken to develop, modify, or enhance a product, service or system; it has a specific beginning and end date. **Project Managers** balance competing demands and mitigate risks to ensure the delivery of an acceptable product to stakeholders and the project sponsor that is within budget, scope, time and quality standards. The levels of **Project Managers** are distinguished by the depth and breadth of the knowledge areas that they must apply to successfully manage a project or portfolio of projects. **Project Managers I and II** generally manage projects of small to medium scope, or assist with larger projects. **Project Managers II** may direct a small project management office.

SUBJECT OF EXAMINATION

The written test is designed to test for knowledge, skills, and/or abilities in such areas as:

1. **Project Management** - These questions test for the primary project management knowledge areas across all phases of the project management life cycle. The major project management knowledge areas are: Integration Management, Scope Management, Time Management, Cost Management, Quality Management, Human Resources Management, Communications Management, Risk Management, and Procurement Management. The phases of the project management life cycle are: Origination, Initiation, Planning, Execution and Control, and Closeout. These questions may also include activity definition and sequencing, cost estimating and tracking, schedule tracking, change control, stakeholder identification and management, quality planning, communications planning, risk identification, and risk monitoring.
2. **Facilitating communications** - These questions test for the principles and practices employed by a facilitator to obtain information, to gain consensus, and/or to promote dialogue between or among individuals or groups to successfully complete a project.
3. **Interviewing** - These questions test for knowledge of the principles and practices employed in obtaining information from individuals through structured conversations. These questions require you to apply the principles, practices, and techniques of effective interviewing to hypothetical interviewing situations. Included are questions that present a problem arising from an interviewing situation, and you must choose the most appropriate course of action to take.
4. **Preparing written material** - These questions test for the ability to present information clearly and accurately, and to organize paragraphs logically and comprehensibly. For some questions, you will be given information in two or three sentences followed by four restatements of the information. You must then choose the best version. For other questions, you will be given paragraphs with their sentences out of order. You must then choose, from four suggestions, the best order for the sentences.
5. **Effectively interacting with agency staff and members of the public** - These questions will test candidates' knowledge of techniques used to interact effectively with a variety of individuals and groups, to provide information about topics of concern, to publicize or clarify agency programs or policies, to negotiate conflicts or resolve complaints, and to represent one's agency or program in a manner in keeping with good public relations practices.

HOW TO TAKE A TEST

I. YOU MUST PASS AN EXAMINATION

A. WHAT EVERY CANDIDATE SHOULD KNOW

Examination applicants often ask us for help in preparing for the written test. What can I study in advance? What kinds of questions will be asked? How will the test be given? How will the papers be graded?

As an applicant for a civil service examination, you may be wondering about some of these things. Our purpose here is to suggest effective methods of advance study and to describe civil service examinations.

Your chances for success on this examination can be increased if you know how to prepare. Those "pre-examination jitters" can be reduced if you know what to expect. You can even experience an adventure in good citizenship if you know why civil service exams are given.

B. WHY ARE CIVIL SERVICE EXAMINATIONS GIVEN?

Civil service examinations are important to you in two ways. As a citizen, you want public jobs filled by employees who know how to do their work. As a job seeker, you want a fair chance to compete for that job on an equal footing with other candidates. The best-known means of accomplishing this two-fold goal is the competitive examination.

Exams are widely publicized throughout the nation. They may be administered for jobs in federal, state, city, municipal, town or village governments or agencies.

Any citizen may apply, with some limitations, such as the age or residence of applicants. Your experience and education may be reviewed to see whether you meet the requirements for the particular examination. When these requirements exist, they are reasonable and applied consistently to all applicants. Thus, a competitive examination may cause you some uneasiness now, but it is your privilege and safeguard.

C. HOW ARE CIVIL SERVICE EXAMS DEVELOPED?

Examinations are carefully written by trained technicians who are specialists in the field known as "psychological measurement," in consultation with recognized authorities in the field of work that the test will cover. These experts recommend the subject matter areas or skills to be tested; only those knowledges or skills important to your success on the job are included. The most reliable books and source materials available are used as references. Together, the experts and technicians judge the difficulty level of the questions.

Test technicians know how to phrase questions so that the problem is clearly stated. Their ethics do not permit "trick" or "catch" questions. Questions may have been tried out on sample groups, or subjected to statistical analysis, to determine their usefulness.

Written tests are often used in combination with performance tests, ratings of training and experience, and oral interviews. All of these measures combine to form the best-known means of finding the right person for the right job.

II. HOW TO PASS THE WRITTEN TEST

A. NATURE OF THE EXAMINATION

To prepare intelligently for civil service examinations, you should know how they differ from school examinations you have taken. In school you were assigned certain definite pages to read or subjects to cover. The examination questions were quite detailed and usually emphasized memory. Civil service exams, on the other hand, try to discover your present ability to perform the duties of a position, plus your potentiality to learn these duties. In other words, a civil service exam attempts to predict how successful you will be. Questions cover such a broad area that they cannot be as minute and detailed as school exam questions.

In the public service similar kinds of work, or positions, are grouped together in one "class." This process is known as *position-classification*. All the positions in a class are paid according to the salary range for that class. One class title covers all of these positions, and they are all tested by the same examination.

B. FOUR BASIC STEPS

1) Study the announcement

How, then, can you know what subjects to study? Our best answer is: "Learn as much as possible about the class of positions for which you've applied." The exam will test the knowledge, skills and abilities needed to do the work.

Your most valuable source of information about the position you want is the official exam announcement. This announcement lists the training and experience qualifications. Check these standards and apply only if you come reasonably close to meeting them.

The brief description of the position in the examination announcement offers some clues to the subjects which will be tested. Think about the job itself. Review the duties in your mind. Can you perform them, or are there some in which you are rusty? Fill in the blank spots in your preparation.

Many jurisdictions preview the written test in the exam announcement by including a section called "Knowledge and Abilities Required," "Scope of the Examination," or some similar heading. Here you will find out specifically what fields will be tested.

2) Review your own background

Once you learn in general what the position is all about, and what you need to know to do the work, ask yourself which subjects you already know fairly well and which need improvement. You may wonder whether to concentrate on improving your strong areas or on building some background in your fields of weakness. When the announcement has specified "some knowledge" or "considerable knowledge," or has used adjectives like "beginning principles of…" or "advanced … methods," you can get a clue as to the number and difficulty of questions to be asked in any given field. More questions, and hence broader coverage, would be included for those subjects which are more important in the work. Now weigh your strengths and weaknesses against the job requirements and prepare accordingly.

3) Determine the level of the position

Another way to tell how intensively you should prepare is to understand the level of the job for which you are applying. Is it the entering level? In other words, is this the position in which beginners in a field of work are hired? Or is it an intermediate or advanced level? Sometimes this is indicated by such words as "Junior" or "Senior" in the class title. Other jurisdictions use Roman numerals to designate the level – Clerk I, Clerk II, for example. The word "Supervisor" sometimes appears in the title. If the level is not indicated by the title, check the description of duties. Will you be working under very close supervision, or will you have responsibility for independent decisions in this work?

4) Choose appropriate study materials

Now that you know the subjects to be examined and the relative amount of each subject to be covered, you can choose suitable study materials. For beginning level jobs, or even advanced ones, if you have a pronounced weakness in some aspect of your training, read a modern, standard textbook in that field. Be sure it is up to date and has general coverage. Such books are normally available at your library, and the librarian will be glad to help you locate one. For entry-level positions, questions of appropriate difficulty are chosen -- neither highly advanced questions, nor those too simple. Such questions require careful thought but not advanced training.

If the position for which you are applying is technical or advanced, you will read more advanced, specialized material. If you are already familiar with the basic principles of your field, elementary textbooks would waste your time. Concentrate on advanced textbooks and technical periodicals. Think through the concepts and review difficult problems in your field.

These are all general sources. You can get more ideas on your own initiative, following these leads. For example, training manuals and publications of the government agency which employs workers in your field can be useful, particularly for technical and professional positions. A letter or visit to the government department involved may result in more specific study suggestions, and certainly will provide you with a more definite idea of the exact nature of the position you are seeking.

III. KINDS OF TESTS

Tests are used for purposes other than measuring knowledge and ability to perform specified duties. For some positions, it is equally important to test ability to make adjustments to new situations or to profit from training. In others, basic mental abilities not dependent on information are essential. Questions which test these things may not appear as pertinent to the duties of the position as those which test for knowledge and information. Yet they are often highly important parts of a fair examination. For very general questions, it is almost impossible to help you direct your study efforts. What we can do is to point out some of the more common of these general abilities needed in public service positions and describe some typical questions.

1) General information

Broad, general information has been found useful for predicting job success in some kinds of work. This is tested in a variety of ways, from vocabulary lists to questions about current events. Basic background in some field of work, such as sociology or economics, may be sampled in a group of questions. Often these are principles which have become familiar to most persons through exposure rather than through formal training. It is difficult to advise you how to study for these questions; being alert to the world around you is our best suggestion.

2) Verbal ability

An example of an ability needed in many positions is verbal or language ability. Verbal ability is, in brief, the ability to use and understand words. Vocabulary and grammar tests are typical measures of this ability. Reading comprehension or paragraph interpretation questions are common in many kinds of civil service tests. You are given a paragraph of written material and asked to find its central meaning.

3) Numerical ability

Number skills can be tested by the familiar arithmetic problem, by checking paired lists of numbers to see which are alike and which are different, or by interpreting charts and graphs. In the latter test, a graph may be printed in the test booklet which you are asked to use as the basis for answering questions.

4) Observation

A popular test for law-enforcement positions is the observation test. A picture is shown to you for several minutes, then taken away. Questions about the picture test your ability to observe both details and larger elements.

5) Following directions

In many positions in the public service, the employee must be able to carry out written instructions dependably and accurately. You may be given a chart with several columns, each column listing a variety of information. The questions require you to carry out directions involving the information given in the chart.

6) Skills and aptitudes

Performance tests effectively measure some manual skills and aptitudes. When the skill is one in which you are trained, such as typing or shorthand, you can practice. These tests are often very much like those given in business school or high school courses. For many of the other skills and aptitudes, however, no short-time preparation can be made. Skills and abilities natural to you or that you have developed throughout your lifetime are being tested.

Many of the general questions just described provide all the data needed to answer the questions and ask you to use your reasoning ability to find the answers. Your best preparation for these tests, as well as for tests of facts and ideas, is to be at your physical and mental best. You, no doubt, have your own methods of getting into an exam-taking mood and keeping "in shape." The next section lists some ideas on this subject.

IV. KINDS OF QUESTIONS

Only rarely is the "essay" question, which you answer in narrative form, used in civil service tests. Civil service tests are usually of the short-answer type. Full instructions for answering these questions will be given to you at the examination. But in case this is your first experience with short-answer questions and separate answer sheets, here is what you need to know:

1) Multiple-choice Questions

Most popular of the short-answer questions is the "multiple choice" or "best answer" question. It can be used, for example, to test for factual knowledge, ability to solve problems or judgment in meeting situations found at work.

A multiple-choice question is normally one of three types—
- It can begin with an incomplete statement followed by several possible endings. You are to find the one ending which *best* completes the statement, although some of the others may not be entirely wrong.
- It can also be a complete statement in the form of a question which is answered by choosing one of the statements listed.

- It can be in the form of a problem – again you select the best answer.

Here is an example of a multiple-choice question with a discussion which should give you some clues as to the method for choosing the right answer:

When an employee has a complaint about his assignment, the action which will *best* help him overcome his difficulty is to
- A. discuss his difficulty with his coworkers
- B. take the problem to the head of the organization
- C. take the problem to the person who gave him the assignment
- D. say nothing to anyone about his complaint

In answering this question, you should study each of the choices to find which is best. Consider choice "A" – Certainly an employee may discuss his complaint with fellow employees, but no change or improvement can result, and the complaint remains unresolved. Choice "B" is a poor choice since the head of the organization probably does not know what assignment you have been given, and taking your problem to him is known as "going over the head" of the supervisor. The supervisor, or person who made the assignment, is the person who can clarify it or correct any injustice. Choice "C" is, therefore, correct. To say nothing, as in choice "D," is unwise. Supervisors have and interest in knowing the problems employees are facing, and the employee is seeking a solution to his problem.

2) True/False Questions

The "true/false" or "right/wrong" form of question is sometimes used. Here a complete statement is given. Your job is to decide whether the statement is right or wrong.

SAMPLE: A roaming cell-phone call to a nearby city costs less than a non-roaming call to a distant city.

This statement is wrong, or false, since roaming calls are more expensive.

This is not a complete list of all possible question forms, although most of the others are variations of these common types. You will always get complete directions for answering questions. Be sure you understand *how* to mark your answers – ask questions until you do.

V. RECORDING YOUR ANSWERS

Computer terminals are used more and more today for many different kinds of exams.

For an examination with very few applicants, you may be told to record your answers in the test booklet itself. Separate answer sheets are much more common. If this separate answer sheet is to be scored by machine – and this is often the case – it is highly important that you mark your answers correctly in order to get credit.

An electronic scoring machine is often used in civil service offices because of the speed with which papers can be scored. Machine-scored answer sheets must be marked with a pencil, which will be given to you. This pencil has a high graphite content which responds to the electronic scoring machine. As a matter of fact, stray dots may register as answers, so do not let your pencil rest on the answer sheet while you are pondering the correct answer. Also, if your pencil lead breaks or is otherwise defective, ask for another.

Since the answer sheet will be dropped in a slot in the scoring machine, be careful not to bend the corners or get the paper crumpled.

The answer sheet normally has five vertical columns of numbers, with 30 numbers to a column. These numbers correspond to the question numbers in your test booklet. After each number, going across the page are four or five pairs of dotted lines. These short dotted lines have small letters or numbers above them. The first two pairs may also have a "T" or "F" above the letters. This indicates that the first two pairs only are to be used if the questions are of the true-false type. If the questions are multiple choice, disregard the "T" and "F" and pay attention only to the small letters or numbers.

Answer your questions in the manner of the sample that follows:

32. The largest city in the United States is
    A. Washington, D.C.
    B. New York City
    C. Chicago
    D. Detroit
    E. San Francisco

1) Choose the answer you think is best. (New York City is the largest, so "B" is correct.)
2) Find the row of dotted lines numbered the same as the question you are answering. (Find row number 32)
3) Find the pair of dotted lines corresponding to the answer. (Find the pair of lines under the mark "B.")
4) Make a solid black mark between the dotted lines.

VI. BEFORE THE TEST

Common sense will help you find procedures to follow to get ready for an examination. Too many of us, however, overlook these sensible measures. Indeed, nervousness and fatigue have been found to be the most serious reasons why applicants fail to do their best on civil service tests. Here is a list of reminders:

- Begin your preparation early – Don't wait until the last minute to go scurrying around for books and materials or to find out what the position is all about.
- Prepare continuously – An hour a night for a week is better than an all-night cram session. This has been definitely established. What is more, a night a week for a month will return better dividends than crowding your study into a shorter period of time.
- Locate the place of the exam – You have been sent a notice telling you when and where to report for the examination. If the location is in a different town or otherwise unfamiliar to you, it would be well to inquire the best route and learn something about the building.
- Relax the night before the test – Allow your mind to rest. Do not study at all that night. Plan some mild recreation or diversion; then go to bed early and get a good night's sleep.
- Get up early enough to make a leisurely trip to the place for the test – This way unforeseen events, traffic snarls, unfamiliar buildings, etc. will not upset you.
- Dress comfortably – A written test is not a fashion show. You will be known by number and not by name, so wear something comfortable.

- Leave excess paraphernalia at home – Shopping bags and odd bundles will get in your way. You need bring only the items mentioned in the official notice you received; usually everything you need is provided. Do not bring reference books to the exam. They will only confuse those last minutes and be taken away from you when in the test room.
- Arrive somewhat ahead of time – If because of transportation schedules you must get there very early, bring a newspaper or magazine to take your mind off yourself while waiting.
- Locate the examination room – When you have found the proper room, you will be directed to the seat or part of the room where you will sit. Sometimes you are given a sheet of instructions to read while you are waiting. Do not fill out any forms until you are told to do so; just read them and be prepared.
- Relax and prepare to listen to the instructions
- If you have any physical problem that may keep you from doing your best, be sure to tell the test administrator. If you are sick or in poor health, you really cannot do your best on the exam. You can come back and take the test some other time.

VII. AT THE TEST

The day of the test is here and you have the test booklet in your hand. The temptation to get going is very strong. Caution! There is more to success than knowing the right answers. You must know how to identify your papers and understand variations in the type of short-answer question used in this particular examination. Follow these suggestions for maximum results from your efforts:

1) Cooperate with the monitor

The test administrator has a duty to create a situation in which you can be as much at ease as possible. He will give instructions, tell you when to begin, check to see that you are marking your answer sheet correctly, and so on. He is not there to guard you, although he will see that your competitors do not take unfair advantage. He wants to help you do your best.

2) Listen to all instructions

Don't jump the gun! Wait until you understand all directions. In most civil service tests you get more time than you need to answer the questions. So don't be in a hurry. Read each word of instructions until you clearly understand the meaning. Study the examples, listen to all announcements and follow directions. Ask questions if you do not understand what to do.

3) Identify your papers

Civil service exams are usually identified by number only. You will be assigned a number; you must not put your name on your test papers. Be sure to copy your number correctly. Since more than one exam may be given, copy your exact examination title.

4) Plan your time

Unless you are told that a test is a "speed" or "rate of work" test, speed itself is usually not important. Time enough to answer all the questions will be provided, but this does not mean that you have all day. An overall time limit has been set. Divide the total time (in minutes) by the number of questions to determine the approximate time you have for each question.

5) Do not linger over difficult questions

If you come across a difficult question, mark it with a paper clip (useful to have along) and come back to it when you have been through the booklet. One caution if you do this – be sure to skip a number on your answer sheet as well. Check often to be sure that you have not lost your place and that you are marking in the row numbered the same as the question you are answering.

6) Read the questions

Be sure you know what the question asks! Many capable people are unsuccessful because they failed to *read* the questions correctly.

7) Answer all questions

Unless you have been instructed that a penalty will be deducted for incorrect answers, it is better to guess than to omit a question.

8) Speed tests

It is often better NOT to guess on speed tests. It has been found that on timed tests people are tempted to spend the last few seconds before time is called in marking answers at random – without even reading them – in the hope of picking up a few extra points. To discourage this practice, the instructions may warn you that your score will be "corrected" for guessing. That is, a penalty will be applied. The incorrect answers will be deducted from the correct ones, or some other penalty formula will be used.

9) Review your answers

If you finish before time is called, go back to the questions you guessed or omitted to give them further thought. Review other answers if you have time.

10) Return your test materials

If you are ready to leave before others have finished or time is called, take ALL your materials to the monitor and leave quietly. Never take any test material with you. The monitor can discover whose papers are not complete, and taking a test booklet may be grounds for disqualification.

VIII. EXAMINATION TECHNIQUES

1) Read the general instructions carefully. These are usually printed on the first page of the exam booklet. As a rule, these instructions refer to the timing of the examination; the fact that you should not start work until the signal and must stop work at a signal, etc. If there are any *special* instructions, such as a choice of questions to be answered, make sure that you note this instruction carefully.

2) When you are ready to start work on the examination, that is as soon as the signal has been given, read the instructions to each question booklet, underline any key words or phrases, such as *least, best, outline, describe* and the like. In this way you will tend to answer as requested rather than discover on reviewing your paper that you *listed without describing*, that you selected the *worst* choice rather than the *best* choice, etc.

3) If the examination is of the objective or multiple-choice type – that is, each question will also give a series of possible answers: A, B, C or D, and you are called upon to select the best answer and write the letter next to that answer on your answer paper – it is advisable to start answering each question in turn. There may be anywhere from 50 to 100 such questions in the three or four hours allotted and you can see how much time would be taken if you read through all the questions before beginning to answer any. Furthermore, if you come across a question or group of questions which you know would be difficult to answer, it would undoubtedly affect your handling of all the other questions.

4) If the examination is of the essay type and contains but a few questions, it is a moot point as to whether you should read all the questions before starting to answer any one. Of course, if you are given a choice – say five out of seven and the like – then it is essential to read all the questions so you can eliminate the two that are most difficult. If, however, you are asked to answer all the questions, there may be danger in trying to answer the easiest one first because you may find that you will spend too much time on it. The best technique is to answer the first question, then proceed to the second, etc.

5) Time your answers. Before the exam begins, write down the time it started, then add the time allowed for the examination and write down the time it must be completed, then divide the time available somewhat as follows:
   - If 3-1/2 hours are allowed, that would be 210 minutes. If you have 80 objective-type questions, that would be an average of 2-1/2 minutes per question. Allow yourself no more than 2 minutes per question, or a total of 160 minutes, which will permit about 50 minutes to review.
   - If for the time allotment of 210 minutes there are 7 essay questions to answer, that would average about 30 minutes a question. Give yourself only 25 minutes per question so that you have about 35 minutes to review.

6) The most important instruction is to *read each question* and make sure you know what is wanted. The second most important instruction is to *time yourself properly* so that you answer every question. The third most important instruction is to *answer every question*. Guess if you have to but include something for each question. Remember that you will receive no credit for a blank and will probably receive some credit if you write something in answer to an essay question. If you guess a letter – say "B" for a multiple-choice question – you may have guessed right. If you leave a blank as an answer to a multiple-choice question, the examiners may respect your feelings but it will not add a point to your score. Some exams may penalize you for wrong answers, so in such cases *only*, you may not want to guess unless you have some basis for your answer.

7) Suggestions
   a. Objective-type questions
      1. Examine the question booklet for proper sequence of pages and questions
      2. Read all instructions carefully
      3. Skip any question which seems too difficult; return to it after all other questions have been answered
      4. Apportion your time properly; do not spend too much time on any single question or group of questions

5. Note and underline key words – *all, most, fewest, least, best, worst, same, opposite,* etc.
6. Pay particular attention to negatives
7. Note unusual option, e.g., unduly long, short, complex, different or similar in content to the body of the question
8. Observe the use of "hedging" words – *probably, may, most likely,* etc.
9. Make sure that your answer is put next to the same number as the question
10. Do not second-guess unless you have good reason to believe the second answer is definitely more correct
11. Cross out original answer if you decide another answer is more accurate; do not erase until you are ready to hand your paper in
12. Answer all questions; guess unless instructed otherwise
13. Leave time for review

   b. Essay questions
   1. Read each question carefully
   2. Determine exactly what is wanted. Underline key words or phrases.
   3. Decide on outline or paragraph answer
   4. Include many different points and elements unless asked to develop any one or two points or elements
   5. Show impartiality by giving pros and cons unless directed to select one side only
   6. Make and write down any assumptions you find necessary to answer the questions
   7. Watch your English, grammar, punctuation and choice of words
   8. Time your answers; don't crowd material

8) Answering the essay question

Most essay questions can be answered by framing the specific response around several key words or ideas. Here are a few such key words or ideas:

M's: manpower, materials, methods, money, management
P's: purpose, program, policy, plan, procedure, practice, problems, pitfalls, personnel, public relations
   a. Six basic steps in handling problems:
   1. Preliminary plan and background development
   2. Collect information, data and facts
   3. Analyze and interpret information, data and facts
   4. Analyze and develop solutions as well as make recommendations
   5. Prepare report and sell recommendations
   6. Install recommendations and follow up effectiveness

   b. Pitfalls to avoid
   1. *Taking things for granted* – A statement of the situation does not necessarily imply that each of the elements is necessarily true; for example, a complaint may be invalid and biased so that all that can be taken for granted is that a complaint has been registered

2. *Considering only one side of a situation* – Wherever possible, indicate several alternatives and then point out the reasons you selected the best one
3. *Failing to indicate follow up* – Whenever your answer indicates action on your part, make certain that you will take proper follow-up action to see how successful your recommendations, procedures or actions turn out to be
4. *Taking too long in answering any single question* – Remember to time your answers properly

IX. AFTER THE TEST

Scoring procedures differ in detail among civil service jurisdictions although the general principles are the same. Whether the papers are hand-scored or graded by machine we have described, they are nearly always graded by number. That is, the person who marks the paper knows only the number – never the name – of the applicant. Not until all the papers have been graded will they be matched with names. If other tests, such as training and experience or oral interview ratings have been given, scores will be combined. Different parts of the examination usually have different weights. For example, the written test might count 60 percent of the final grade, and a rating of training and experience 40 percent. In many jurisdictions, veterans will have a certain number of points added to their grades.

After the final grade has been determined, the names are placed in grade order and an eligible list is established. There are various methods for resolving ties between those who get the same final grade – probably the most common is to place first the name of the person whose application was received first. Job offers are made from the eligible list in the order the names appear on it. You will be notified of your grade and your rank as soon as all these computations have been made. This will be done as rapidly as possible.

People who are found to meet the requirements in the announcement are called "eligibles." Their names are put on a list of eligible candidates. An eligible's chances of getting a job depend on how high he stands on this list and how fast agencies are filling jobs from the list.

When a job is to be filled from a list of eligibles, the agency asks for the names of people on the list of eligibles for that job. When the civil service commission receives this request, it sends to the agency the names of the three people highest on this list. Or, if the job to be filled has specialized requirements, the office sends the agency the names of the top three persons who meet these requirements from the general list.

The appointing officer makes a choice from among the three people whose names were sent to him. If the selected person accepts the appointment, the names of the others are put back on the list to be considered for future openings.

That is the rule in hiring from all kinds of eligible lists, whether they are for typist, carpenter, chemist, or something else. For every vacancy, the appointing officer has his choice of any one of the top three eligibles on the list. This explains why the person whose name is on top of the list sometimes does not get an appointment when some of the persons lower on the list do. If the appointing officer chooses the second or third eligible, the No. 1 eligible does not get a job at once, but stays on the list until he is appointed or the list is terminated.

X. HOW TO PASS THE INTERVIEW TEST

The examination for which you applied requires an oral interview test. You have already taken the written test and you are now being called for the interview test – the final part of the formal examination.

You may think that it is not possible to prepare for an interview test and that there are no procedures to follow during an interview. Our purpose is to point out some things you can do in advance that will help you and some good rules to follow and pitfalls to avoid while you are being interviewed.

What is an interview supposed to test?

The written examination is designed to test the technical knowledge and competence of the candidate; the oral is designed to evaluate intangible qualities, not readily measured otherwise, and to establish a list showing the relative fitness of each candidate – as measured against his competitors – for the position sought. Scoring is not on the basis of "right" and "wrong," but on a sliding scale of values ranging from "not passable" to "outstanding." As a matter of fact, it is possible to achieve a relatively low score without a single "incorrect" answer because of evident weakness in the qualities being measured.

Occasionally, an examination may consist entirely of an oral test – either an individual or a group oral. In such cases, information is sought concerning the technical knowledges and abilities of the candidate, since there has been no written examination for this purpose. More commonly, however, an oral test is used to supplement a written examination.

Who conducts interviews?

The composition of oral boards varies among different jurisdictions. In nearly all, a representative of the personnel department serves as chairman. One of the members of the board may be a representative of the department in which the candidate would work. In some cases, "outside experts" are used, and, frequently, a businessman or some other representative of the general public is asked to serve. Labor and management or other special groups may be represented. The aim is to secure the services of experts in the appropriate field.

However the board is composed, it is a good idea (and not at all improper or unethical) to ascertain in advance of the interview who the members are and what groups they represent. When you are introduced to them, you will have some idea of their backgrounds and interests, and at least you will not stutter and stammer over their names.

What should be done before the interview?

While knowledge about the board members is useful and takes some of the surprise element out of the interview, there is other preparation which is more substantive. It *is* possible to prepare for an oral interview – in several ways:

1) Keep a copy of your application and review it carefully before the interview

This may be the only document before the oral board, and the starting point of the interview. Know what education and experience you have listed there, and the sequence and dates of all of it. Sometimes the board will ask you to review the highlights of your experience for them; you should not have to hem and haw doing it.

2) Study the class specification and the examination announcement

Usually, the oral board has one or both of these to guide them. The qualities, characteristics or knowledges required by the position sought are stated in these documents. They offer valuable clues as to the nature of the oral interview. For example, if the job involves supervisory responsibilities, the announcement will usually indicate that knowledge of modern supervisory methods and the qualifications of the candidate as a supervisor will be tested. If so, you can expect such questions, frequently in the form of a hypothetical situation which you are expected to solve. NEVER go into an oral without knowledge of the duties and responsibilities of the job you seek.

3) Think through each qualification required
Try to visualize the kind of questions you would ask if you were a board member. How well could you answer them? Try especially to appraise your own knowledge and background in each area, *measured against the job sought*, and identify any areas in which you are weak. Be critical and realistic – do not flatter yourself.

4) Do some general reading in areas in which you feel you may be weak
For example, if the job involves supervision and your past experience has NOT, some general reading in supervisory methods and practices, particularly in the field of human relations, might be useful. Do NOT study agency procedures or detailed manuals. The oral board will be testing your understanding and capacity, not your memory.

5) Get a good night's sleep and watch your general health and mental attitude
You will want a clear head at the interview. Take care of a cold or any other minor ailment, and of course, no hangovers.

What should be done on the day of the interview?
Now comes the day of the interview itself. Give yourself plenty of time to get there. Plan to arrive somewhat ahead of the scheduled time, particularly if your appointment is in the fore part of the day. If a previous candidate fails to appear, the board might be ready for you a bit early. By early afternoon an oral board is almost invariably behind schedule if there are many candidates, and you may have to wait. Take along a book or magazine to read, or your application to review, but leave any extraneous material in the waiting room when you go in for your interview. In any event, relax and compose yourself.

The matter of dress is important. The board is forming impressions about you – from your experience, your manners, your attitude, and your appearance. Give your personal appearance careful attention. Dress your best, but not your flashiest. Choose conservative, appropriate clothing, and be sure it is immaculate. This is a business interview, and your appearance should indicate that you regard it as such. Besides, being well groomed and properly dressed will help boost your confidence.

Sooner or later, someone will call your name and escort you into the interview room. *This is it.* From here on you are on your own. It is too late for any more preparation. But remember, you asked for this opportunity to prove your fitness, and you are here because your request was granted.

What happens when you go in?
The usual sequence of events will be as follows: The clerk (who is often the board stenographer) will introduce you to the chairman of the oral board, who will introduce you to the other members of the board. Acknowledge the introductions before you sit down. Do not be surprised if you find a microphone facing you or a stenotypist sitting by. Oral interviews are usually recorded in the event of an appeal or other review.

Usually the chairman of the board will open the interview by reviewing the highlights of your education and work experience from your application – primarily for the benefit of the other members of the board, as well as to get the material into the record. Do not interrupt or comment unless there is an error or significant misinterpretation; if that is the case, do not hesitate. But do not quibble about insignificant matters. Also, he will usually ask you some question about your education, experience or your present job – partly to get you to start talking and to establish the interviewing "rapport." He may start the actual questioning, or turn it over to one of the other members. Frequently, each member undertakes the questioning on a particular area, one in which he is perhaps most competent, so you can expect each member to participate in the examination. Because time is limited, you may also expect some rather abrupt switches in the direction the questioning takes, so do not be upset by it. Normally, a board member will not pursue a single line of questioning unless he discovers a particular strength or weakness.

After each member has participated, the chairman will usually ask whether any member has any further questions, then will ask you if you have anything you wish to add. Unless you are expecting this question, it may floor you. Worse, it may start you off on an extended, extemporaneous speech. The board is not usually seeking more information. The question is principally to offer you a last opportunity to present further qualifications or to indicate that you have nothing to add. So, if you feel that a significant qualification or characteristic has been overlooked, it is proper to point it out in a sentence or so. Do not compliment the board on the thoroughness of their examination – they have been sketchy, and you know it. If you wish, merely say, "No thank you, I have nothing further to add." This is a point where you can "talk yourself out" of a good impression or fail to present an important bit of information. Remember, *you close the interview yourself*.

The chairman will then say, "That is all, Mr. _____, thank you." Do not be startled; the interview is over, and quicker than you think. Thank him, gather your belongings and take your leave. Save your sigh of relief for the other side of the door.

How to put your best foot forward

Throughout this entire process, you may feel that the board individually and collectively is trying to pierce your defenses, seek out your hidden weaknesses and embarrass and confuse you. Actually, this is not true. They are obliged to make an appraisal of your qualifications for the job you are seeking, and they want to see you in your best light. Remember, they must interview all candidates and a non-cooperative candidate may become a failure in spite of their best efforts to bring out his qualifications. Here are 15 suggestions that will help you:

1) **Be natural – Keep your attitude confident, not cocky**

If you are not confident that you can do the job, do not expect the board to be. Do not apologize for your weaknesses, try to bring out your strong points. The board is interested in a positive, not negative, presentation. Cockiness will antagonize any board member and make him wonder if you are covering up a weakness by a false show of strength.

2) **Get comfortable, but don't lounge or sprawl**

Sit erectly but not stiffly. A careless posture may lead the board to conclude that you are careless in other things, or at least that you are not impressed by the importance of the occasion. Either conclusion is natural, even if incorrect. Do not fuss with your clothing, a pencil or an ashtray. Your hands may occasionally be useful to emphasize a point; do not let them become a point of distraction.

3) **Do not wisecrack or make small talk**

This is a serious situation, and your attitude should show that you consider it as such. Further, the time of the board is limited – they do not want to waste it, and neither should you.

4) Do not exaggerate your experience or abilities

In the first place, from information in the application or other interviews and sources, the board may know more about you than you think. Secondly, you probably will not get away with it. An experienced board is rather adept at spotting such a situation, so do not take the chance.

5) If you know a board member, do not make a point of it, yet do not hide it

Certainly you are not fooling him, and probably not the other members of the board. Do not try to take advantage of your acquaintanceship – it will probably do you little good.

6) Do not dominate the interview

Let the board do that. They will give you the clues – do not assume that you have to do all the talking. Realize that the board has a number of questions to ask you, and do not try to take up all the interview time by showing off your extensive knowledge of the answer to the first one.

7) Be attentive

You only have 20 minutes or so, and you should keep your attention at its sharpest throughout. When a member is addressing a problem or question to you, give him your undivided attention. Address your reply principally to him, but do not exclude the other board members.

8) Do not interrupt

A board member may be stating a problem for you to analyze. He will ask you a question when the time comes. Let him state the problem, and wait for the question.

9) Make sure you understand the question

Do not try to answer until you are sure what the question is. If it is not clear, restate it in your own words or ask the board member to clarify it for you. However, do not haggle about minor elements.

10) Reply promptly but not hastily

A common entry on oral board rating sheets is "candidate responded readily," or "candidate hesitated in replies." Respond as promptly and quickly as you can, but do not jump to a hasty, ill-considered answer.

11) Do not be peremptory in your answers

A brief answer is proper – but do not fire your answer back. That is a losing game from your point of view. The board member can probably ask questions much faster than you can answer them.

12) Do not try to create the answer you think the board member wants

He is interested in what kind of mind you have and how it works – not in playing games. Furthermore, he can usually spot this practice and will actually grade you down on it.

13) Do not switch sides in your reply merely to agree with a board member

Frequently, a member will take a contrary position merely to draw you out and to see if you are willing and able to defend your point of view. Do not start a debate, yet do not surrender a good position. If a position is worth taking, it is worth defending.

14) Do not be afraid to admit an error in judgment if you are shown to be wrong

The board knows that you are forced to reply without any opportunity for careful consideration. Your answer may be demonstrably wrong. If so, admit it and get on with the interview.

15) Do not dwell at length on your present job

The opening question may relate to your present assignment. Answer the question but do not go into an extended discussion. You are being examined for a *new* job, not your present one. As a matter of fact, try to phrase ALL your answers in terms of the job for which you are being examined.

Basis of Rating

Probably you will forget most of these "do's" and "don'ts" when you walk into the oral interview room. Even remembering them all will not ensure you a passing grade. Perhaps you did not have the qualifications in the first place. But remembering them will help you to put your best foot forward, without treading on the toes of the board members.

Rumor and popular opinion to the contrary notwithstanding, an oral board wants you to make the best appearance possible. They know you are under pressure – but they also want to see how you respond to it as a guide to what your reaction would be under the pressures of the job you seek. They will be influenced by the degree of poise you display, the personal traits you show and the manner in which you respond.

ABOUT THIS BOOK

This book contains tests divided into Examination Sections. Go through each test, answering every question in the margin. We have also attached a sample answer sheet at the back of the book that can be removed and used. At the end of each test look at the answer key and check your answers. On the ones you got wrong, look at the right answer choice and learn. Do not fill in the answers first. Do not memorize the questions and answers, but understand the answer and principles involved. On your test, the questions will likely be different from the samples. Questions are changed and new ones added. If you understand these past questions you should have success with any changes that arise. Tests may consist of several types of questions. We have additional books on each subject should more study be advisable or necessary for you. Finally, the more you study, the better prepared you will be. This book is intended to be the last thing you study before you walk into the examination room. Prior study of relevant texts is also recommended. NLC publishes some of these in our Fundamental Series. Knowledge and good sense are important factors in passing your exam. Good luck also helps. So now study this Passbook, absorb the material contained within and take that knowledge into the examination. Then do your best to pass that exam.

EXAMINATION SECTION

SAMPLE TEST

PRINCIPLES AND PRACTICES OF PROGRAM PLANNING AND PROJECT MANAGEMENT

Test material will be presented in a multiple-choice question format.

Test Task: You will be presented with situations in which you must apply knowledge of program planning and project management in order to answer the questions correctly.

SAMPLE QUESTION:
Which one of the following is developed by the project manager to clearly define the boundaries of a project by detailing the product, deliverables, and major objectives?

- A. cost baseline
- B. scope statement
- C. risk management plan
- D. quality management plan

The correct answer to this sample question is Choice B.

Solution:

Choice A is not correct. A cost baseline is a time-phased budget that a project manager prepares to monitor and measure cost performance throughout the project life cycle. It does not define the product, deliverables, or major objectives of the project.

Choice B is the correct answer to this question. The scope statement is developed by the project manager to define the project boundaries by outlining the product, deliverables, and major objectives.

Choice C is not correct. A risk management plan is a document that a project manager prepares to foresee risks, estimate impacts, and define responses to issues. It does not define the product, deliverables, or major objectives of the project.

Choice D is not correct. A quality management plan is a document that a project manager prepares to define the acceptable level of quality, which is typically defined by the customer, and to describe how the project will ensure this level of quality in its deliverables and work processes. It does not define the product, deliverables, or major objectives of the project.

EXAMINATION SECTION
TEST 1

DIRECTIONS: Each question or incomplete statement is followed by several suggested answers or completions. Select the one that BEST answers the question or completes the statement. *PRINT THE LETTER OF THE CORRECT ANSWER IN THE SPACE AT THE RIGHT.*

1. _____ is commonly used to report on project performance.
   A. Earned Value Management
   B. WBS
   C. Quality Management Plan
   D. RBS

   1._____

2. Which of the following is NOT a process associated with communications management?
   A. Distribute information
   B. Manage stakeholder expectations
   C. Plan communication
   D. Survey questionnaire

   2._____

3. As a project manager, you are expected to make relevant information available to project stakeholders as planned. Which process does this relate to?
   A. Distribute information
   B. Manage stakeholder expectations
   C. Plan communication
   D. Report performance

   3._____

4. Report performance involves all of the following EXCEPT
   A. collecting and distributing performance data
   B. collecting and distributing progress measurements
   C. collecting stakeholder information needs
   D. collecting and distributing forecasts

   4._____

5. Of the following examples listed, which is a sign of feedback from the receiver?
   A. No written response from the receiver
   B. An acknowledgement or additional questions from the receiver
   C. Encoding the message by the receiver
   D. Decoding the message by the receiver

   5._____

6. As a project manager you are expected to create a scope statement. Once you have the statement, you find it to be useful in all the following ways EXCEPT
   A. describing the purpose of the project
   B. describing the objectives of the project
   C. distributing information
   D. explaining the business problems the project is expected to solve

   6._____

7. What are project deliverables?
    A. Tangible products that the project is expected to deliver
    B. Prioritized list of deliverables
    C. Project scope statement
    D. Project documents

8. As a project manager, you are arranging criteria for project completion criteria. You could organize it using all of the following EXCEPT
    A. functional department
    B. milestones
    C. tasks of projects
    D. project phase

9. Which of the following is not a task under "Developing human resource plan"?
    A. Documenting organizational relationships
    B. Looking for the availability of required human resources
    C. Identification and documentation of project roles and responsibilities
    D. Creating a staffing plan

10. If you are a project manager who is keen in managing a project team, you would undertake any of the following EXCEPT
    A. creating a staffing plan
    B. evaluating individual team member performance
    C. providing feedback
    D. resolving conflicts

11. Nurturing the team is a vital role of a project manager. If you have to do so, what would you avoid?
    A. Guide the team members as required
    B. Provide mentoring throughout the project
    C. Remove the team member who is found to be less skilled
    D. On-the-job training

12. War room creation is an example of
    A. co-location
    B. management skills
    C. rewards and recognitions
    D. establishing ground rules

13. The team member roles and responsibilities could be documented using all of the following EXCEPT
    A. functional chart
    B. text-oriented format
    C. hierarchical type organizational chart
    D. matrix-based responsibility chart

14. _____ is NOT an example of constraints placed upon the project by current organizational policies.
    A. Hiring freeze
    B. Reduced training funds
    C. Organizational chart templates
    D. Rewards and Increments Freeze

15. As a project manager, you have decided to have a virtual team. What kind of limitation would this create with regards to team development?
    A. Rewards and recognition
    B. Establishing ground rules
    C. Team building
    D. Co-location

16. Unplanned training means
    A. team building using virtual team arrangement
    B. competencies developed as a result of project performance appraisals
    C. on-the-job training
    D. training that is done without any planning in advance

17. Resource break down structure is an example of
    A. functional chart
    B. text-oriented format
    C. hierarchical type organizational chart
    D. matrix-based responsibility chart

18. A project manager would consider the following as inputs to define scope EXCEPT
    A. requirements document
    B. project Charter
    C. product management plan
    D. organizational process charts

19. Aldo is a project manager and has to terminate a project earlier than planned. The level and extent of completion should be documented. Under which is this done?
    A. Verify scope
    B. Create scope
    C. Control scope
    D. Define scope

20. Sam, an IT project manager, is having difficulty in getting resources for his project, and hence has to depend highly on department heads. Which type of organization is Sam most likely working with?
    A. Functional
    B. Tight matrix
    C. Weak matrix
    D. Projectized

Questions 21-25.

Len is a project manager of an infrastructure project manager of a well-known company. He is involved in various processes of scope management. Look at the following chart and align the different processes to various tasks listed. Choose the appropriate answer for each process and list them under corresponding tasks.

	Processes	Corresponding tasks	List of tasks
21.	Define scope	21._____	A. Monitoring project scope and project status
22.	Control scope	22._____	B. Defining and documenting stakeholder needs
23.	Collect requirements	23._____	C. Formalizing acceptance of the complete project deliverables
24.	Verify scope	24._____	D. Breaking down the project into smaller, more manageable tasks
25.	Create WBS	25._____	E. Developing a detailed description of the project and its ultimate product

---

KEY (CORRECT ANSWERS)

1. A	11. C	21. E
2. D	12. A	22. A
3. A	13. A	23. B
4. C	14. C	24. C
5. B	15. D	25. D
6. C	16. B	
7. A	17. C	
8. C	18. C	
9. B	19. A	
10. A	20. A	

TEST 2

DIRECTIONS: Each question or incomplete statement is followed by several suggested answers or completions. Select the one that BEST answers the question or completes the statement. *PRINT THE LETTER OF THE CORRECT ANSWER IN THE SPACE AT THE RIGHT.*

1. In which of the following processes would risk be identified? 1.____
   A. Risk identification
   B. Risk monitoring and control
   C. Qualitative risk analysis
   D. Risk identification, monitoring and control

2. Jack has prepared a risk management plan for his project and also identified risks in his project. Which of the following processes should Jack do next? 2.____
   A. Plan risk responses
   B. Perform qualitative analysis
   C. Perform quantitative analysis
   D. Monitor and control risk

3. Which of the following is NOT a step in risk management? 3.____
   A. Perform qualitative analysis
   B. Monitor and control risk
   C. Risk identification
   D. Risk breakdown structure

4. Sue is a project manager for an IT project at a corporate office. She is engaged in the process of identifying risks. To do so, she collects inputs from experts from the field through a questionnaire. What is this technique called? 4.____
   A. Interview
   B. Documentation review
   C. Delphi technique
   D. Register risk

5. Positive risks may be responded by which of the following: 5.____
      I. Exploit   II. Accept   III. Mitigate   IV. Share

   A. I and III
   B. All of the above
   C. I, II and IV
   D. I, II and III

6. Risk _____ is a response to negative risks. 6.____
   A. identification
   B. mitigation
   C. response plan
   D. management plan

7. Which of the following statements is NOT true about risk management?
    A. Risk register documents all the risks in detail
    B. Risks always have negative impacts and not positive
    C. Risk mitigation is a response to negative risks
    D. Risk register documents the risks in detail

8. _____ is the document that lists all the risks in a hierarchical fashion.
    A. Risk breakdown structure
    B. Lists of risks
    C. Risk management plan
    D. Monte Carlo diagram

9. Nicole is a project manager of a reforestation project. In one of the project reviews, she realizes that a risk has occurred. Which document should Nicole refer to take an appropriate action?
    A. Risk response plan
    B. Risk register
    C. Risk management plan
    D. Risk breakdown structure

10. As a project manager, you have invited experts for an effective brainstorming session to identify risks involved in the project. What is the ideal group size?
    A. 3   B. 6   C. 4   D. 5

11. Of the following personnel, who is NOT involved in project risk identification activities?
    A. Clerical staff
    B. Subject matter experts
    C. Other project managers
    D. Risk management experts

12. _____ is one of the tools/techniques used in risk identification.
    A. Risk tracker
    B. Checklist analysis
    C. Risk register
    D. Project scope

13. Jim is a project manager in a bank. He is collecting input for the risk identification process. What input would he be collecting to identify risks?
    I. Project scope statement
    II. Enterprise environmental factors
    III. Project management plan
    IV. Diagramming techniques

    A. I and IV only
    B. III and IV only
    C. All of the above
    D. I, II and III only

14. Which of the following could a project manager collect from a risk tracker?
    I. Root causes of risk and updated risk categories
    II. List of identified risks
    III. Risk register
    IV. List of potential responses

    A. I and IV only
    B. III and IV only
    C. I, II and IV
    D. II only

15. The risk management plan should describe the entire risk management process, including auditing of the process, and should also define _____.
    A. reporting
    B. environmental factors
    C. organizational process assets
    D. project management plan

16. What do risk categories define?
    A. How to communicate risk activities and their results
    B. Types and sources of risks
    C. How risk management will be done on the process
    D. When and how the risk management activities appear in the project schedule

17. Which of the following is not a method of risk identification?
    A. Diagramming
    B. Interviewing
    C. SWOT
    D. RBS

18. Shauna is conducting a qualitative risk analysis for her project. What is she required to do?
    A. Apply a numerical rating to each risk
    B. Assess the probability and impact of each identified risk
    C. Assign each major risk to a risk owner
    D. Outline a course of action for each major risk identified

19. Which of the following is not a criterion to close a risk?
    A. Risk is no longer valid
    B. Risk event has occurred
    C. Risk activities are recorded regularly
    D. Risk closure at the direction of a project manager

20. As a project manager, you establish a risk contingency budget. Which of the following is not a purpose of establishing a risk contingency budget?
    A. To be reviewed as a standing agenda item for project team meetings
    B. To prepare in advance to manage the risks successfully
    C. To have some reserve funds
    D. To avoid going over the budget allotted

21. Which of the following statements is NOT correct in terms of designing a risk management?
    A. Risk is inherent to project work
    B. In any organization, projects will have common risks
    C. Some risks may occur more than once in the life a project
    D. Risks identified will definitely occur

22. All identified potential risk events that are viewed to be relevant to the project are to be recorded using the
    A. risk register
    B. risk management matrix
    C. risk report
    D. SOW

23. _____ is/are an example of a business risk.
    A. Poorly understood requirements
    B. A merger
    C. Introduction of new technology to the organization
    D. Work outside the project scope

24. Personnel turnover in a project is a
    A. Business risk
    B. Not a risk at all
    C. Technology risk
    D. Project risk

25. Which of the following is not an example of mitigation?
    A. Set expectations
    B. Involve customer in early planning process
    C. Provide training for personnel
    D. Hiring a backup person for a key team member

KEY (CORRECT ANSWERS)

1. D
2. B
3. D
4. C
5. C

6. B
7. B
8. A
9. A
10. A

11. A
12. B
13. D
14. C
15. A

16. B
17. D
18. B
19. C
20. A

21. D
22. B
23. B
24. D
25. D

TEST 3

DIRECTIONS: Each question or incomplete statement is followed by several suggested answers of completions. Select the one that best answers the question or complete the statement. *PRINT THE LETTER OF THE CORRECT ANSWER IN THE SPACE AT THE RIGHT.*

1. Project cost management deals with all the following EXCEPT:
    A. Estimating costs
    B. Budgeting
    C. Controlling costs
    D. Communicating costs

    1.____

2. Which of the following is not a process associated with project cost management?
    A. Control costs
    B. Maintain reserves
    C. Estimate costs
    D. Determine budget

    2.____

3. _____ is not a key deliverable of project cost processes.
    A. Cost performance baseline
    B. Activity cost estimates
    C. Results of estimates
    D. Work performance measurements

    3.____

4. As a project manager, you are calculating depreciation for an object. You are doing this by depreciating the same amount from the cost each year.
    What kind of depreciation technique are you applying?
    A. Sum of year depreciation
    B. Double-declining balance
    C. Multiple depreciation
    D. Straight line depreciation

    4.____

5. Which of the following is not a characteristic of analogous estimating?
    A. It is a top-down approach
    B. It is a form of an expert judgment
    C. It makes less time when compared to bottom-up estimation
    D. It is more accurate when compared to bottom-up estimation

    5.____

6. CPI = EV/AC. If CPI is less than 1, the project
    A. is over the budget
    B. is within the budget
    C. would be left over with unused budget
    D. efficiency is less

    6.____

7. Which of the following is not a tool used for estimating cost?
    A. Cost of quality
    B. Expert judgment
    C. Two point estimates
    D. Three point estimates

    7.____

8. What are the traditional project management triple constraints?
    A. Time, cost, resources
    B. Scope, cost, resources
    C. Scope, time, cost
    D. Resources, scope, budget

    8.____

9. Sam, an IT project manager, is having difficulty getting resources for his project, and hence has to depend highly on department heads.
   Which type of organization is Sam most likely working with?
   A. Functional
   B. Tight Matrix
   C. Weak Matrix
   D. Projectized

10. After-project costs are called _____.
    A. cost of quality
    B. extra costs
    C. life cycle costs
    D. over budget costs

11. Critical chain is a tool and technique for _____.
    A. developing schedule process
    B. defining critical path
    C. sequencing activities process
    D. estimating activity duration

12. The following are outputs for sequencing activities:
    A. Project schedule network diagram, Milestone list
    B. Project document updates, Project schedule network diagram
    C. Project schedule, Project document updates
    D. Schedule data, Schedule baseline

13. The schedule performance index is a measure of:
    A. Difference between earned value and planned value
    B. Ratio between earned value and planned value
    C. Difference between earned value and estimate at completion
    D. Ratio between estimate at completion and earned value

14. Which of the following is not an input, output or tools and technique for control schedule process?
    A. Project schedule, work performance measurements and variance analysis
    B. Project management plan, project document updates and schedule compression
    C. Work performance information, schedule baseline and schedule data
    D. Project schedule, change requests and resource leveling

15. Contracts, resource calendar, risk register and forecasts are all termed as
    A. inputs to administer procurements process
    B. outputs from close procurements process
    C. project documents
    D. tools and techniques of conduct procurement process

16. Fast tracking can be best described as
    A. one of the schedule compression techniques
    B. adding resources to activities on critical path
    C. shared or critical resources available only at specific times
    D. performing activities in parallel to shorten project duration

17. Which of the following contract types places the highest risk on the seller?
    A. Cost plus fixed fee
    B. Firm fixed price
    C. Cost plus incentive fee
    D. Time and material

18. Using the Power/Interest grid, a stakeholder with low power and having high interest on the project should be
    A. monitored
    B. managed closely
    C. kept satisfied
    D. kept informed

19. Stakeholder classification information is found in which of the following documents?
    A. Communications management plan
    B. Stakeholder register
    C. Stakeholder management strategy document
    D. Human resource plan

20. Thomas is a project manager of a well-reputed organization. One of your senior managers approaches you to explain constraints on labor utilization followed by a request to delay a couple of your projects. What is the best way to approach this situation?
    A. Agree with the senior manager and delay a couple of your projects
    B. Perform an impact analysis of the requested change
    C. Report the situation to the senior management and make a complaint against the senior manager
    D. Disagree with the senior manager and continue with the progress of the projects managed by you

21. Project management is defined as
    A. completion of a project
    B. gaining trust of the people involved in the project
    C. completing a WBS
    D. the application of specific knowledge, skills and tools

22. The most common form of dependency is
    A. Start to Start
    B. Finish to Start
    C. Finish to Finish
    D. Start to Finish

23. Kelly is a project manager who is in phase of project evaluation. Which of the following has to be considered during project evaluation phase?
    I.   Give feedback to team members
    II. Learn from experiences
    III. Monitor
    IV. Celebrate

The correct answer(s) is/are:
- A. I only
- B. I, IV and III
- C. III only
- D. I, II and IV

24. Which of the following are very vital for the implementation of the project, and also must be repeated over and over during project's life.
    - I.   Correct
    - II. Monitor
    - III. Estimate time and cost
    - IV. Analyze

    The correct answer(s) is/are:
    - A. I, II and III
    - B. III only
    - C. I, III and IV
    - D. I, II and IV

25. What is the average amount of time is to be allocated to project planning?
    - A. 10%
    - B. 25%
    - C. 22%
    - D. 2%

KEY (CORRECT ANSWERS)

1. D
2. B
3. C
4. C
5. D

6. A
7. C
8. C
9. A
10. C

11. A
12. B
13. B
14. C
15. C

16. D
17. B
18. D
19. B
20. B

21. D
22. B
23. D
24. D
25. A

TEST 4

DIRECTIONS: Each question or incomplete statement is followed by several suggested answers of completions. Select the one that best answers the question or complete the statement. *PRINT THE LETTER OF THE CORRECT ANSWER IN THE SPACE AT THE RIGHT.*

1. Imagine you are assigned a project for which you do not have the required competency and experience to manage. What is the best plan of action?
    A. Make sure that you disclose any areas of improvement that need to be immediately addressed with the project sponsor before accepting the assignment
    B. Do not inform anyone about the gaps and learn as much as you can before any critical activity is due for delivery
    C. Consider the opportunity as a stepping stone for your career development and accept it
    D. Tell your boss that you cannot manage as you do not have the relevant experience and decline it

1.____

2. You are the project manager of a new project and are involved in selecting a vendor for acquiring products required for the project. Your close friend is running a company that is also very competitive and a reputed one along with other vendors who are competing for the bid. How can you handle this situation?
    A. Do not participate in the vendor selection process as this may be considered a conflict of interest
    B. Provide information to help your friend get the contract as you are the project manager of the project
    C. Do not inform anyone about your personal contact and be involved in the vendor selection process as normal
    D. Discuss with your project sponsor the possibility of a conflict of interest and leave the decision to him on the next steps

2.____

3. You have provided good guidance to your team members and this has resulted in successful execution of all of the phases involved. There was a particular phase that has been identified as very critical and the presence of a technical expert helped achieve this success. In the senior management review meeting you were credited with the success of the project, with specific mention of that particular phase. What do you do in this situation?
    A. Accept the appreciation and feel proud about the success of the project
    B. Do not mention anything about the technical expert role as you were the project manager for this project
    C. Give credit to the technical expert and let the senior management know how the presence of the technical expert helped the team to be successful
    D. Accept the appreciation from the senior management and thank the technical expert in private for achieving this success

3.____

4. As a project manager you are preparing status reports for a meeting with the stakeholders. One of your team members has come out with an issue that will cause some delay in the project timeline. You have a plan that can be implemented to make sure that this issue can be managed without causing any delay in the timeline, but you currently do not have the time to update the project plan. How will you handle this situation?   4._____
    A. Present the status of the project as *on-track* without discussing anything about this issue as you will have time to prepare before the next meeting
    B. Cancel the meeting as you do not have the time to update the details to be provided to the stakeholders
    C. Present the status of the project *as-is* without minimizing the effect of the delay and discuss details of the planned approach to solve this issue
    D. Fire your team that is responsible for causing this delay as it has created a bad impression of you amongst the stakeholders

5. John is an Associate Director in a pharmaceutical company managing its internal projects. He has presented whitepapers on project execution methodologies and is highly respected within the organization. He also regularly conducts workshops & lectures in coordination with PMO. What kind of power does John possess?   5._____
    A. Referent power   C. Reward power
    B. Coercive power   D. Expert power

6. You are a project manager working for a non-profit organization. You had been assigned a project that is in the initial stage and involves development of an eco-system in a large community. You are reviewing the deliverables and templates from similar projects that are available in the company lessons learnt knowledge base. Which item will be of much importance to you?   6._____
    A. Project Information Management System
    B. Enterprise Environmental Factors
    C. Organization Process Assets
    D. Standard Templates

7. A project that you were managing is nearing completion. As part of the deliverables you are required to complete lessons-learned documentation of the project. What is the primary purpose of creating lessons-learned documentation?   7._____
    A. Provide information of project success
    B. Help identify all the failures
    C. Provide information on minimizing negative impacts and maximizing positive events for future projects of similar nature
    D. Comply with the organization's objectives

8. You are managing project teams that work from different locations and there has been issues with the teams' ability to effectively perform. This has resulted in delay in timeline. Which kind of team development technique would be most effective in this situation?   8._____
    A. Mediation   C. Co-location
    B. Training   D. Rewards

9. The project sponsor has requested that you create a project charter for a new project that you will manage next month. Which document will you utilize to create the project charter that will justify the need for the project?   9._____
    A. Project SOW   C. Business Case
    B. Business Need   D. Cost-benefit Analysis

10. An audit is being performed by a team for the project you are managing. The team reports that the standards utilized need to be analyzed as several processes that are not relevant to the current project.
    What is the process that the team is currently involved?
    - A. Quality planning
    - B. Quality control
    - C. Quality assurance
    - D. Benchmark creation

11. The change control board of your organization has approved changes that were submitted and the project team is executing them.
    What would this process be considered?
    - A. Executing the change request
    - B. Implementing a corrective action
    - C. Gold-plating
    - D. Approving the change request

12. Which is the primary technique that is carried out to ensure that a contract award is executed correctly or not?
    - A. Litigation
    - B. Contract negotiation
    - C. Inspections
    - D. Procurement audit

13. In the final stages of completing a project, you and your team are involved in creating the project report that will be presented to the stakeholders. Which of the following information is not appropriate to be included in the final report?
    - A. Recommendations from your team
    - B. Project success factors
    - C. WBS dictionary
    - D. Details of the process improvements

14. At the completion of a project, your team has completed the lessons-learned documentation and archived in the database. Who should have access to these documents?
    - A. Project team members
    - B. Operations department
    - C. All of the company's members
    - D. Functional managers

15. You are project manager for a large project that is in the final stages of completion and you need to formally provide information on the major milestone achieved. You are also in need of immediate feedback from the stakeholders. Which is the best communication method to meet this requirement?
    - A. E-mail
    - B. Web publishing
    - C. Meeting
    - D. Videoconferencing

16. Which document will formally authorize a project manager to start the project?
    - A. Project SOW
    - B. Project Charter
    - C. Business Case
    - D. Stakeholder Register

17. Which of the following documents would be utilized to ascertain the project's investment worthiness?
    - A. Project Charter
    - B. Business Case
    - C. Business Need
    - D. Procurement documents

18. Which of the following conflict resolution is considered as Lose-lose solution?
    A. Problem-solving
    B. Forcing
    C. Compromising
    D. Withdrawing

19. McGregor's Theory states that all workers fit into one of the two groups. Which of the following theories believes that people are willing to work on their own and need less supervision?
    A. Theory X
    B. Theory Y
    C. Maslow's Hierarchy
    D. Expectancy

20. The major cause for conflicts on a project are schedule, project priorities and _____.
    A. cost
    B. resources
    C. personality
    D. management

21. The project manager is responsible for
    A. the success of the project
    B. achieving the project objectives
    C. authorizing the project
    D. performing the project work

22. Which of the following actions correspond to reducing the consequences of future problems?
    A. Corrective action
    B. Preventive action
    C. Defect repair
    D. Change request

23. As a project manager for a large-scale project, you are in the process of procuring materials required for the project. Which of the following documents will you not be responsible for?
    A. Procurement documents
    B. Procurement statements of work
    C. Source selection criteria
    D. Proposals

24. During which process group will the detailed requirements be gathered?
    A. Initiating
    B. Planning
    C. Executing
    D. Closing

25. The values that illustrate PMIs code of ethics and professional conduct are
    A. respect, honesty, responsibility and honorability
    B. honesty, cultural diversity, integrity and responsibility
    C. fairness, responsibility, honesty and respect
    D. honorability, fairness, respect and responsibility

KEY (CORRECT ANSWERS)

1. A
2. D
3. C
4. C
5. D

6. C
7. C
8. C
9. C
10. C

11. A
12. D
13. C
14. C
15. D

16. B
17. B
18. C
19. B
20. B

21. B
22. B
23. D
24. B
25. C

EXAMINATION SECTION
TEST 1

DIRECTIONS: Each question or incomplete statement is followed by several suggested answers of completions. Select the one that BEST answers the question or Complete the statement. *PRINT THE LETTER OF THE CORRECT ANSWER IN THE SPACE AT THE RIGHT.*

1. An accepted deadline for a project approaches. However, the project manager realizes only 85% of the work has been completed. The project manager then issues a change request.
   What should the change request authorize?

   A. Corrective action based on causes
   B. Escalation approval to use contingency funding
   C. Additional resources using the contingency fund
   D. Team overtime to meet schedule

   1.____

2. _____ is a valid tool or technique to assist the project manager to assure the success of the process improvement plan.

   A. Benchmarking
   B. Change control system
   C. Process analysis
   D. Configuration management system

   2.____

3. A project manager meets with the project team to review lessons learned from previous projects. In what activity is the team involved?

   A. Performance management
   B. Project team status meeting
   C. Scope identification
   D. Risk identification

   3.____

4. _____ process helps you to purchase goods from external suppliers.

   A. Quality management
   B. Procurement management
   C. Cost management
   D. Communication management

   4.____

5. Which of the following is not involved in procurement management?

   A. Review supplier performance against contract
   B. Identify and resolve supplier performance issues
   C. Communicate the status to management
   D. Manage a WBS

   5.____

6. _____ contract is advantageous to a buyer.

   A. Fixed price
   B. Cost reimbursable
   C. Time and material
   D. Fixed price plus incentive

   6.____

7. Which of the following contracts is advantageous to a seller?

    A. Fixed price
    B. Cost reimbursable
    C. Time and material
    D. Fixed price plus incentive

8. Tom is a manager of a project whose deliverable has many uncertainties associated with it. What kind of contract should he use during the procurement process?

    A. Fixed price
    B. Cost reimbursable
    C. Time and material
    D. Fixed price plus incentive

9. Cost plus _____ is not a cost-reimbursable contract.

    A. fixed fee
    B. fee
    C. fixed time
    D. incentive fee

10. _____ type of contract helps both the seller and buyer to save, if the performance criteria are exceeded.

    A. Cost plus fixed fee
    B. Cost plus fee
    C. Cost plus fixed time
    D. Cost plus incentive fee

11. A project manager with a construction company. She has to complete a project in a specified time, but does have enough time to send the job out for bids. What type of contract would save her time?

    A. Fixed price
    B. Cost reimbursable
    C. Time and material
    D. Fixed price plus incentive

12. The major type(s) of standard warranty (ies) that are used in the business environment is (are):

    A. express
    B. negotiated
    C. implied
    D. A and C

13. During contract management, the project manager must consider the

    A. acquisition process and contract administration
    B. contract administration and ecological environment
    C. ecological environment and acquisition process
    D. offer, acceptance and consideration

14. Which contract type places the most risk on the seller?   14._____

    A. Cost plus percentage fee
    B. Cost plus incentive fee
    C. Cost plus fixed fee
    D. Firm fixed price

15. Finalizing project close-out happens when a project manager   15._____

    A. archives the project records
    B. completes the contract
    C. complete lessons learned
    D. reassigns the team

16. Unit price contract is fair to both owner and contractor,   16._____

    A. as the actual volumes will be measured and paid as the work proceeds
    B. as the owner will provide bill of quantities
    C. as both are absorbing an equal amount of risk
    D. all of the above

17. Bill is the manager of a project that requires different areas of expertise.   17._____
    Which one of the following contracts should he sign?

    A. Fixed price
    B. Cost reimbursable
    C. Time and material
    D. Unit price

18. Which of the following contracts is commonly used in projects that involve pilot   18._____
    programs or harness new technologies?

    A. Fixed price
    B. Incentive
    C. Time and material
    D. Unit price

19. Procurement cycle involves all of the following steps EXCEPT   19._____

    A. supplier contract
    B. renewal
    C. sending a proposal
    D. information gathering

20. What would happen if a project manager does not take up a background review during the   20._____
    procurement process?

    A. Price might not be negotiated
    B. Credibility of the goods might not be validated
    C. Goods might not be shipped
    D. Both A and B

21. _____ is not a part of a procurement document.

    A. Buyer's commencement to the bid
    B. Summons by the financially responsible party
    C. Establishing terms and conditions of a contract
    D. Roles of responsibilities of internal team

22. Which of the following is NOT an example of a procurement document?

    A. Offers
    B. Contracts
    C. Project record archives
    D. Request for quotation

23. A project manager needs to follow _____ for a good procurement document to be drafted.

    A. clear definition of the responsibilities, rights and commitments of both parties in the contract
    B. clear definition of the nature and quality of the goods or services to be provided
    C. clear and easy to understand language
    D. all of the above

24. Which of the following is not a concern with respect to procurement management?

    A. Reassigning the team
    B. Not all goods and services that a business requires need to be purchased from outside
    C. You would need to have a good idea of what you exactly require and then go on to consider various options and alternatives
    D. You would need to consider different criteria, apart from just the cost, to finally decide on which supplier you would want to go with.

25. Source qualifications are a part of the _____ phase of Acquisition Process Cycle.

    A. post-award
    B. pre-award
    C. award
    D. origination

KEY (CORRECT ANSWERS)

1. A	11. C
2. C	12. D
3. D	13. A
4. B	14. D
5. D	15. B
6. A	16. C
7. B	17. D
8. B	18. B
9. C	19. C
10. D	20. B

21. D
22. C
23. D
24. A
25. C

TEST 2

DIRECTIONS: Each question or incomplete statement is followed by several suggested answers of completions. Select the one that BEST answers the question or Complete the statement. *PRINT THE LETTER OF THE CORRECT ANSWER IN THE SPACE AT THE RIGHT.*

1. Which of the following project tools details the project scope? 1._____

    A. Project plan
    B. Gantt chart
    C. Milestone checklist
    D. Score cards

2. Which of the following is NOT a project tool? 2._____

    A. Gantt chart
    B. Milestone checklist
    C. Score cards
    D. MS project

3. _____ is accompanied by project audits by a third party. As a result, non-compliance and action items are tracked. 3._____

    A. Gantt chart
    B. Milestone checklist
    C. Project reviews
    D. Delivery reviews

4. An IT project manager, is involved in tracking his team's performance. Which tool would he use to gauge this performance? 4._____

    A. Score cards
    B. Gantt chart
    C. Project management software
    D. Milestone checklist

5. What tool does a manager use to track the interdependencies of each project activity? 5._____

    A. Project plan
    B. Gantt chart
    C. Project management software
    D. Milestone checklist

6. Which tool would be used for a manager to determine if he or she is on track in terms of project progress? 6._____

    A. Project management software
    B. Delivery reviews
    C. Project reviews
    D. Milestone checklist

7. Which of the following tools is used for individual member promotion? 7._____

    A. Delivery reviews
    B. Score cards
    C. Project reviews
    D. Milestone checklist

8. Which of the following is NOT a project management process? 8._____

    A. Project planning
    B. Project initiation
    C. Project management software
    D. Closeout and evaluation

9. _____ is the phase in which the service provider proves the eligibility and ability of completing the project to the client. 9._____

    A. Pre-sale period
    B. Project execution
    C. Sign-off
    D. Closeout and evaluation

10. Controlling of the project could be done by following all of the following protocols EXCEPT 10._____

    A. communication plan
    B. quality assurance test plan
    C. test plan
    D. project plan

11. A manager wants his project to be successful and hence verifies the successful outcome of every activity leading to successful completion of the project. Which of the following activities would he use to do so? 11._____

    A. Control
    B. Test plan
    C. Project plan
    D. Validation

12. What happens during the closeout and evaluation phase? 12._____

    A. Evaluation of the entire project
    B. Hand over the implemented system
    C. Identifying mistakes and taking necessary action
    D. All of the above

13. A project manager, is conducting validation and verification functions. Which team's assistance would she need in order to do so? 13._____

    A. Quality assurance team
    B. Project team
    C. Client team
    D. Third-party vendor

14. Tracking the effort and cost of the project is done during _____.

    A. project execution
    B. control and validation
    C. closeout and evaluation
    D. communication plan

15. _____ is the entity created for governing the processes, practices, tools and other activities related to project management in an organization.

    A. Project management office
    B. Project management software
    C. Quality assurance
    D. None of the above

16. A project management office must be built with the following considerations EXCEPT

    A. process optimization
    B. productivity enhancement
    C. building the bottom line of their organization
    D. none of the above

17. An advantage of a project management office is that it

    A. helps cut down staff
    B. helps cut down resources
    C. refines the processes related to project management
    D. all of the above

18. A project management office could fail because of

    A. lack of executive management support
    B. incapability
    C. it adds figures to the bottom line of the company
    D. both A and B

19. _____ is used to analyze the difficulties that may arise due to the execution of the project.

    A. Project management office
    B. Project management triangle
    C. Both A and B
    D. None of the above

20. The three constraints in a project management triangle are _____.

    A. time, cost and scope
    B. time, resources and quality
    C. time, resources and people
    D. time, resources and cost

21. A project manager, is experiencing challenges related to project triangle and hence finds difficulty in achieving the project objectives. Which of the following skills would help her?

    A. Time management
    B. Effective communication
    C. Managing people
    D. All of the above

22. _____ is NOT a role of a project manager.

    A. Carrying out basic project tasks
    B. Keeping stakeholders informed on the project progress
    C. Defining project scope and assigning tasks to team members
    D. Setting objectives

23. Kathy is advising Nicole on the goals and challenges a project manager must consider. Which of the following should she discuss?

    A. Deadlines
    B. Client satisfaction
    C. No budget overrun
    D. All of the above

24. Team management deals with all of the following EXCEPT

    A. providing incentives and encouragement
    B. maintaining warm and friendly relationship with teammates
    C. meeting requirements of the client
    D. including them in project related decisions

25. _____ is vital to win client satisfaction.

    A. Finishing the work on scheduled time
    B. Ensuring that most standards are met
    C. Having a limited relationship with the client
    D. All of the above

KEY (CORRECT ANSWERS)

1. A
2. D
3. C
4. A
5. B

6. D
7. B
8. C
9. A
10. C

11. D
12. D
13. A
14. A
15. A

16. D
17. C
18. D
19. B
20. A

21. D
22. A
23. D
24. C
25. A

TEST 3

DIRECTIONS: Each question or incomplete statement is followed by several suggested answers of completions. Select the one that BEST answers the question or Complete the statement. *PRINT THE LETTER OF THE CORRECT ANSWER IN THE SPACE AT THE RIGHT.*

1. What type of strategy is followed by a manager before his workforce focuses on with performance?

    A. Activators
    B. Behaviors
    C. Consequences
    D. Deviators

    1.____

2. _____ define how the workforce performs or behaves within the activity or situation as a result of activators or consequences.

    A. Deviators
    B. Consequences
    C. Behaviors
    D. Activators

    2.____

3. _____ explain how the manager handles the workforce after the performance.

    A. Deviators
    B. Consequences
    C. Behaviors
    D. Activators

    3.____

4. Which of the following is found to have a great impact on workforce behavior?

    A. Deviators
    B. Consequences
    C. Behaviors
    D. Activators

    4.____

5. Nancy, an IT project manager, is keen to delegate her work. She is aware that a good manager's role is about delegating work effectively in order to complete the task. What should she consider before delegating?

    A. Delegating the work with clear instructions and expectations stated
    B. Providing enough moral support
    C. Identify individuals that are capable of carrying out a particular task
    D. All the above

    5.____

6. Which of the following is NOT a tool related to controlling and assuring quality?

    A. Check sheet
    B. Cause-and-effect diagram
    C. Activators
    D. Scatter diagram

    6.____

7. _____ are used for understanding business, implementation and organizational problems.

    A. Cause-and-effect diagrams
    B. Scatter diagrams
    C. Control charts
    D. Pareto charts

    7.____

8. Jim is replacing the earlier project manager in the middle of the project and hard-pressed with time. He has to work on a priority basis.
Which of the following tools would he use to identify priorities?

   A. Cause-and-effect diagram
   B. Scatter diagram
   C. Control chart
   D. Pareto chart

8.____

Questions 9-11 refer to the following chart.

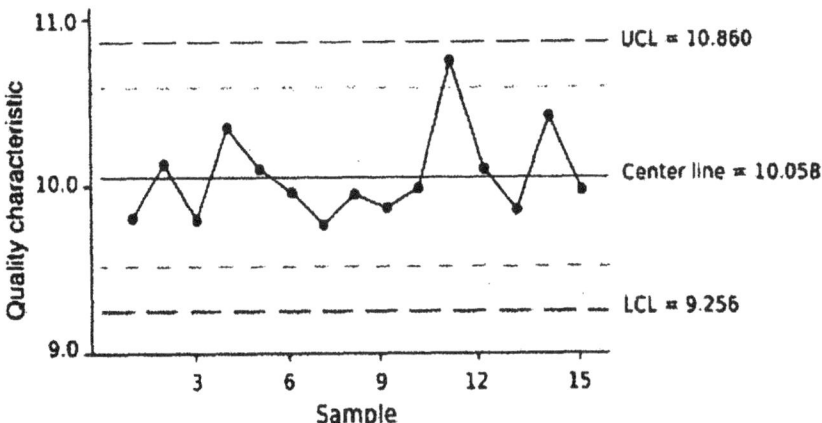

9. What type of tool is this?

   A. Control chart
   B. Flow chart
   C. Scatter diagram
   D. Pareto chart

9.____

10. The above-mentioned chart/tool is used for _____.

    A. identifying sets of priorities
    B. comparing two variables
    C. monitoring the performance of a process
    D. gathering and organizing data

10.____

11. The above chart/tool could be used to identify all of the following EXCEPT

    A. the stability of the process
    B. the common cause of variation
    C. the parameter(s) that have the highest impact on the specific concern
    D. conditions where the monitoring team needs to react

11.____

12. Which of the following tools would a project manager use to perform a trend analysis?

    A. Flow chart
    B. Scatter diagram
    C. Cause-and-effect diagram
    D. Pareto chart

12.____

13. _____ is/are a common and simple method used by project managers to arrive at an effective cause-and-effect diagram.

   A. Survey
   B. Brainstorming
   C. Informal discussions
   D. Formal presentations

13._____

14. Which of the following tools should a project manager use to gain a brief understanding of the project's critical path?

   A. Flow chart
   B. Pareto chart
   C. Histogram
   D. Check sheet

14._____

15. _____ is NOT a step involved in the benchmarking process.

   A. Planning
   B. Analysis of data
   C. Monitoring
   D. None of the above

15._____

16. As a project manager, where will you collect primary data when you collect information?

   i) Benchmarked company
   ii) Press
   iii) Publication
   iv) Website

   A. Only I
   B. Both I and II
   C. I, II, III and IV
   D. Both I and IV

16._____

17. Which of the following methods is recommended to conduct primary research?

   A. E-mail
   B. Referring to the website of other companies
   C. Telephone
   D. Face-to-face interviews

17._____

18. Analysis of data involves all of the following EXCEPT

   A. sharing data with all the stakeholders
   B. data presentation
   C. results projection
   D. classifying the performance gaps in processes

18._____

4 (#3)

19. _____ is referred to as an enabler, which will help project managers to act wisely.   19.____

   A. Projection of results
   B. Performance gap identification
   C. Root cause of performance gaps
   D. Presentation of data

20. Which of the following needs to be done in order to monitor the quality of the project?   20.____

   A. Evaluating the progress made
   B. Reiterating the impact of change
   C. Making necessary adjustments
   D. All the above

Use the following cause-and-effect diagram to answer questions 21 through 23.

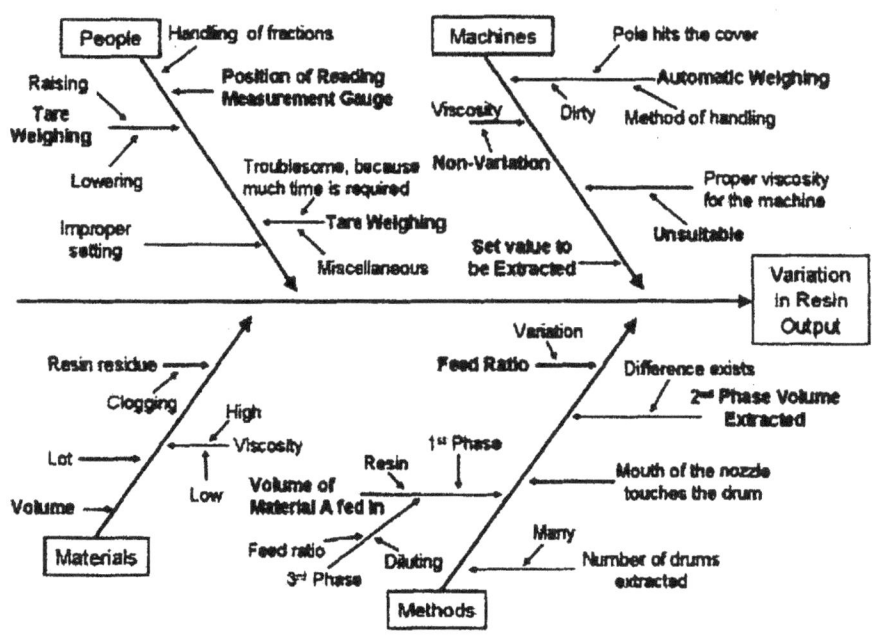

21. Which of the following is NOT represented in this diagram?   21.____

   A. Problem
   B. Major cause of the problem
   C. Contributing factors
   D. Possible causes of the problem

22. What is the effect with respect to the diagram?   22.____

   A. Materials
   B. Methods
   C. Variation in Resin Output
   D. People

23. As a project manager, what will you do to gain a better understanding of the problems and handling them? 23._____

    A. Investigations
    B. Surveys
    C. Interviews
    D. All the above

24. Kotter's change management process involves all the following steps EXCEPT 24._____

    A. building a team
    B. resource management
    C. creating a vision
    D. removing obstacles

25. _____ lets team members know why they are working on a change initiative. 25._____

    A. Removing obstacles
    B. Building a team
    C. Integrating the change
    D. Creating a vision

KEY (CORRECT ANSWERS)

1. A
2. C
3. B
4. B
5. D

6. C
7. A
8. D
9. A
10. C

11. C
12. B
13. B
14. A
15. D

16. C
17. B
18. A
19. C
20. D

21. B
22. C
23. D
24. B
25. D

TEST 4

DIRECTIONS: Each question or incomplete statement is followed by several suggested answers of completions. Select the one that best answers the question or Complete the statement. *PRINT THE LETTER OF THE CORRECT ANSWER IN THE SPACE AT THE RIGHT.*

1. Which of the following is NOT a communication blocker?   1._____
   A. Judging
   B. Accusing
   C. Globalizing
   D. Listening

2. Using words like "always" and "never" is an example of _____.   2._____
   A. judging
   B. accusing
   C. globalizing
   D. listening

3. What should you do as a project manager to eliminate communication blockers?   3._____
   A. Encourage others to avoid communication blockers by educating them
   B. Be aware of the various blockers and take steps to remove them
   C. Model to promote effective and empathetic communication
   D. All of the above

4. What would happen if there were no proper communication channel?   4._____
   A. Inefficient flow of information
   B. Clarity among employees on what is expected of them
   C. Sense of company mind/common vision among employees
   D. Clarity among employees on the happening within the company

5. As a project manager, you could use any one of the following types of language EXCEPT _____ for communicating with your team.   5._____
   A. formal
   B. insulting
   C. informal
   D. unofficial

6. A(n) _____ is/are NOT an example of formal communication.   6._____
   A. annual report
   B. business plan
   C. social gathering
   D. review meetings

7. _____ types of communication are used to communicate company policies, goals and procedures.
   A. Formal
   B. Informal
   C. Unofficial
   D. None of the above

8. _____ is NOT an example of informal communication.
   A. Survey
   B. Quality circle
   C. Team work
   D. Training program

9. "Grapevine" is an example of _____ communication.
   A. Formal
   B. Informal
   C. Unofficial
   D. None of the above

10. What question would you NOT consider as a project manager before choosing the right method to communicate?
    A. Who is the target audience?
    B. Will it lead to employee productivity?
    C. What kind of information would be helpful for clarity among employees?
    D. Which is the best way to threaten the employees?

11. Which of the following is not included in "The Five Ws of Communication Management"?
    A. What information would prompt employees to work out of fear?
    B. What information is essential for the project?
    C. What is the time required for the communication to happen effectively?
    D. Who requires information and what type of information is required?

12. _____ refers to developing a message.
    A. Decoding
    B. Encoding
    C. Transmission
    D. Feedback

13. _____ refers to interpreting the message.
    A. Decoding
    B. Encoding
    C. Transmission
    D. Feedback

14. Which of the following is not necessarily involved in a communication process?
    A. Sender
    B. Transmission
    C. Vision
    D. Receiver

15. _____ is NOT a sign of active listening.
    A. Making eye contact
    B. Asking questions to gain clarity
    C. Using gestures like nodding head
    D. Using gestures that distract the speaker

16. Madeline is a project manager and involved in conflict management. Which of the following should she use to manage a conflict?
    A. Identify actions that resolve conflicts
    B. Identify actions that would aggravate conflicts
    C. Consider different methods of resolving the conflict
    D. All the above

17. A managerial action that would NOT aggravate conflict is _____.
    A. poor communication
    B. assertive style of leadership
    C. ill-defined expectations
    D. authoritative style of leadership

18. An example of a managerial action that would NOT minimize a conflict is
    A. well-defined job descriptions
    B. participative approach
    C. submissive style of leadership
    D. fostering team spirit

19. Which of the following methods could you use as a project manager to handle conflicts?
    A. Flight
    B. Fake
    C. Fight
    D. All of the above

20. _____ is the term used when people run away from problems instead of confronting them and turn to avoidance as a means of handling conflict.
    A. Flight
    B. Fake
    C. Fight
    D. Fold

21. _____ is the term used when an individual is made to agree to a solution by means of browbeating.
    A. Flight
    B. Fake
    C. Fight
    D. Fold

22. Which of the following is NOT a step in conflict management?
    A. Choose the best solution that satisfy most people most of the time and implement this
    B. Engage in participatory dialogue and find a range of solutions that will be acceptable to all the parties concerned
    C. Eliminate those who promote mutual understanding and acceptance
    D. Identify the limiting resource or constraint that is generally at the root cause of the conflict

23. Which of the following is NOT a skill required for conflict resolution?
    A. Clarity in communication
    B. Aggressiveness
    C. Negotiation
    D. Listening

24. _____ is essential to be prepared for any problems that may arise when it is least expected.
    A. Conflict management
    B. Communication management
    C. Crisis management
    D. None of the above

25. Which of the following is NOT a type of crisis?
   A. Financial
   B. Technological
   C. Natural
   D. Negotiation

KEY (CORRECT ANSWERS)

1. D
2. C
3. D
4. A
5. B

6. C
7. A
8. A
9. C
10. D

11. A
12. B
13. A
14. C
15. D

16. D
17. B
18. C
19. D
20. A

21. D
22. C
23. B
24. C
25. D

EXAMINATION SECTION
TEST 1

DIRECTIONS: Each question or incomplete statement is followed by several suggested answers or completions. Select the one that BEST answers the question or completes the statement. *PRINT THE LETTER OF THE CORRECT ANSWER IN THE SPACE AT THE RIGHT.*

1. In many instances, managers deliberately set up procedures and routines that more than one department or more than one employee is required to complete and verify an entire operation or transaction.
   The MAIN reason for establishing such routines is generally to
   A. minimize the chances of gaps and deficiencies in feedback of information to management
   B. expand the individual employee's vision and concern for broader organizational objectives
   C. provide satisfaction of employees' social and egoistic needs through teamwork and horizontal communications
   D. facilitate internal control designed to prevent errors, whether intentional or accidental

    1.____

2. Committees—sometimes referred to as boards, commissions, or task forces—are widely used in government to investigate certain problems or to manage certain agencies.
   Of the following, the MOST serious limitation of the committee approach to management in government is that
   A. it reflects government's inability to delegate authority effectively to individual executives
   B. committee members do not usually have similar backgrounds, experience, and abilities
   C. it promotes horizontal communication at the expense of vertical communication
   D. the spreading out of responsibility to a committee often results in a willingness to settle for weak, compromise solutions

    2.____

3. Of the following, the BEST reason for replacing methods of committees on a staggered or partial basis rather than replacing all members simultaneously is that this practice
   A. gives representatives of different interest groups a chance to contribute their ideas
   B. encourages continuity of policy since retained members are familiar with previous actions
   C. prevents the interpersonal frictions from building up and hindering the work of the group
   D. improves the quality of the group's recommendations and decisions by stimulating development of new ideas

    3.____

4. Assume that in considering a variety of actions to take to solve a given problem, a manager decides to take no action at all.
   According to generally accepted management practice, such a decision would be
   A. *proper*, because under normal circumstances it is better to make no decision
   B. *improper*, because inaction would be rightly construed as shunning one's responsibilities
   C. *proper*, since this would be a decision which might produce more positive results than the other alternatives
   D. *improper*, since such a solution would delay corrective action and exacerbate the problem

5. Some writers in the field of management assume that when a newly promoted manager has been informed by his superior about the subordinates he is to direct and the extent of his authority, that is all that is necessary.
   However, thereafter, this new manager should realize that, for practical purposes, his authority will be effective ONLY when
   A. he accepts full responsibility for the actions of his subordinates
   B. his subordinates are motivated to carry out their assignments
   C. it derives from acceptable personal attributes rather than from his official position
   D. he exercises it in an authoritarian manner

6. A newly appointed manager is assigned to assist the head of a small developing agency handling innovative programs. Although this manager is a diligent worker, he does not delegate authority to middle- and lower-echelon supervisors.
   The MOST important reason why it would be desirable to change this attitude toward delegation is because otherwise
   A. he may have to assume more responsibility for the actions of his subordinates than is implied in the authority delegated to him
   B. his subordinates will tend to produce innovative solutions on their own
   C. the agency will become a decentralized type of organization in which he cannot maintain adequate controls
   D. he may not have time to perform other essential tasks

7. All types of organizations and all functions within them are to varying degrees affected today by the need to understand the application of computer systems to management practices.
   The one of the following purposes for which such systems would be MOST useful is to
   A. lower the costs of problem-solving by utilizing data that is already in the agency's control system correlated with new data
   B. stabilize basic patterns of the organization into long-term structures and relationships
   C. give instant solutions to complex problems
   D. affect savings in labor costs for office tasks involving non-routine complex problems

8. Compared to individual decision-making, group decision-making is burdened with the DISADVANTAGE of
   A. making snap judgments
   B. pressure to examine all relevant elements of the problem
   C. greater motivation needed to implement the decision
   D. the need to clarify problems for the group participants

8.____

9. Assume that a manager in an agency, faced with a major administrative problem, has developed a number of alternative solutions to the problem. Which of the following would be MOST effective in helping the manager make the best decision?
   A. *Experience*, because a manager can distill from the past the fundamental reasons for success or failure since the future generally duplicates the past
   B. *Experimentation*, because it is the method used in scientific inquiry and can be tried out economically in limited areas
   C. *Research analysis*, because it is generally less costly than most other methods and involves the interrelationships among the more critical factors that bear upon the goal sought
   D. *Value forecasting*, because it assigns numerical significance to the values of alternative tangible and intangible choices and indicates the degree of risk involved in each choice

9.____

10. Management information systems operate more effectively for managers than mere data tabulating systems because information systems
    A. eliminate the need for managers to tell information processors what is required
    B. are used primarily for staff rather than line functions
    C. are less expensive to operate than manual methods of data collection
    D. present and utilize data in a meaningful form

10.____

11. Project-type organizations are in widespread use today because they offer a number of advantages.
    The MOST important purpose of the project organization is to
    A. secure a higher degree of coordination than could be obtained in a conventional line structure
    B. provide an orderly way of phrasing projects in and out of organizations
    C. expedite routine administrative processes
    D. allow for rapid assessment of the status of any given project and its effect on agency productivity

11.____

12. A manager adjusts his plans for future activity by reviewing information about the performance of his subordinates.
    This is an application of the process of
    A. human factor impact   B. coordinated response
    C. feedback communication   D. reaction control

12.____

13. From the viewpoint of the manager in an agency, the one of the following which is the MOST constructive function of a status system or a rank system based on employee performance is that the system
    A. makes possible effective communication, thereby lessening social distances between organizational levels
    B. is helpful to employees of lesser ability because it provides them with an incentive to exceed their capacities
    C. encourages the employees to attain or exceed the goals set for them by the organization
    D. diminishes friction in assignment and work relationships of personnel

14. Some managers ask employees who have been newly hired by their agency and then assigned to their divisions or units such questions as: *What are your personal goals? What do you expect from your job? Why do you want to work for this organization?*
    For a manager to ask these questions is GENERALLY considered
    A. *inadvisable*; these questions should have been asked prior to hiring the employee
    B. *inadvisable*; the answers will arouse subjective prejudices in the manager before he sees what kind of work the employee can do
    C. *advisable*; this approach indicates to the employee that the manager is interested in him as an individual
    D. *advisable*; the manager can judge how much of a disparity exists between the employee's goals and the agency's goals

15. Assume that you have prepared a report to your superior recommending a reorganization of your staff to eliminate two levels of supervision. The total number of employees would remain the same, with the supervisors of the two eliminated levels taking on staff assignments.
    In your report, which one of the following should NOT be listed as an expected result of such a reorganization?
    A. Fewer breakdowns and distortions in communications to staff
    B. Greater need for training
    C. Broader opportunities for development of employee skills
    D. Fewer employee errors due to exercise of closer supervision and control

16. *Administration* has often been criticized as being unproductive in the sense that it seems far removed from the end products of an organization.
    According to modern management thought, this criticism, for the most part, is
    A. *invalid*, because administrators make it possible for subordinates to produce goods or services by directing coordination, and controlling their activities
    B. *valid*, because most subordinates usually do the work required to produce goods and services with only general direction from their immediate superiors
    C. *invalid*, because administrators must see to all of the details associated with the production of services
    D. *valid*, because administrators generally work behind the scenes and are mainly concerned with long-range planning

17. A manager must be able to evaluate the relative importance of his decisions and establish priorities for carrying them out.
Which one of the following factors bearing on the relative importance of making a decision would indicate to a manager that he can delegate that decision to a subordinate or give it low priority? The
    A. decision concerns a matter on which strict confidentiality must be maintained
    B. community impact of the decision is great
    C. decision can be easily changed
    D. decision commits the agency to heavy expenditure of funds

17.____

18. Suppose that you are responsible for reviewing and submitting to your superior the monthly reports from ten field auditors. Despite your repeated warnings to these auditors, most of them hand in their reports close to or after the deadline dates, so that you have no time to return them for revision and find yourself working overtime to make the necessary corrections yourself. The deadline dates for the auditors' reports and your report cannot be changed.
Of the following, the MOST probable cause for this continuing situation is that
    A. these auditors need retraining in the writing of this type of report
    B. possible disciplinary action as a result of the delay by the auditors has not been impressed upon them
    C. the auditors have had an opportunity to provide you with feedback to explain the reasons for the delays
    D. you, as the manager, have not used disciplinary measures of sufficient severity to change their behavior

18.____

19. Assume that an agency desiring to try out a *management-by-objectives* program has set down the guidelines listed below to implement this activity. Which one of these guidelines is MOST likely to present obstacles to the success of this type of program?
    A. Specific work objectives should be determined by top management for employees at all levels.
    B. Objectives should be specific, attainable, and preferably measurable as to units, costs, ratios, time, etc.
    C. Standards of performance should be either qualitative or quantitative, preferably quantitative.
    D. There should be recognition and rewards for successful achievement or objectives.

19.____

20. Of the following, the MOST meaningful way to express productivity where employees work a standard number of hours each day is in terms of the relationship between man-
    A. hours expended and number of work-units needed to produce the final product
    B. days expended and goods and services produced
    C. days and energy expended
    D. days expended and number of workers

20.____

21. Agencies often develop productivity indices for many of their activities. 21.____
Of the following, the MOST important use for such indices is generally to
    A. measure the agency's output against its own performance
    B. improve quality standards while letting productivity remain unchanged
    C. compare outputs of the agency with outputs in private industry
    D. determine manpower requirements

22. The MOST outstanding characteristic of staff authority, such as that of a public 22.____
relations officer in an agency, as compared with line authority, is generally
accepted to be
    A. reliance upon personal attributes
    B. direct relationship to the primary objectives of the organization
    C. absence of the right to direct or command
    D. responsibility for attention to technical details

23. In the traditional organization structure, there are often more barriers to 23.____
upward communication than to downward communication.
From the viewpoint of a manager whose goal is to overcome obstacles to
communication, this situation should be
    A. *accepted*; the downward system is the more important since it is highly
       directive, giving necessary orders, instructions, and procedures
    B. *changed*; the upward system should receive more emphasis than the
       downward system, which represents stifling bureaucratic authority
    C. *accepted*; it is generally conceded that upward systems supply enough
       feedback for control purposes necessary to the organization's survival
    D. *changed*; research has generally verified the need for an increase in
       upward communications to supply more information about employees'
       ideas, attitudes, and performance

24. A principal difficulty in productivity measurement for local government services 24.____
is in defining and measuring output, a problem familiar to managers. A
measurement that merely looks good, but which may be against the public
interest, is another serious problem. Managers should avoid encouraging
employees to take actions that lead to such measurements.
In accordance with the foregoing statement, it would be MOST desirable for a
manager to develop a productivity measure that
    A. correlates the actual productivity measure with impact on benefit to the
       citizenry
    B. does not allow for a mandated annual increase in productivity
    C. firmly fixes priorities for resource allocations
    D. uses numerical output, by itself, in productivity incentive plans

25. For a manager, the MOST significant finding of the Hawthorne studies and 25.____
experiments is that an employee's productivity is affected MOST favorably
when the
    A. importance of tasks is emphasized and there is a logical arrangement of
       work functions

B. physical surroundings and work conditions are improved
C. organization has a good public relations program
D. employee is given recognition and allowed to participate in decision-making

KEY (CORRECT ANSWERS)

1.	D		11.	A
2.	D		12.	C
3.	B		13.	C
4.	C		14.	A
5.	B		15.	D
6.	D		16.	A
7.	A		17.	C
8.	D		18.	D
9.	C		19.	A
10.	D		20.	B

21. A
22. C
23. D
24. A
25. D

TEST 2

DIRECTIONS: Each question or incomplete statement is followed by several suggested answers or completions. Select the one that BEST answers the question or completes the statement. *PRINT THE LETTER OF THE CORRECT ANSWER IN THE SPACE AT THE RIGHT.*

1. Which one of the following is generally accepted by managers as the MOST difficult aspect of a training program in staff supervision?
   A. Determining training needs of the staff
   B. Evaluating the effectiveness of the courses
   C. Locating capable instructors to teach the courses
   D. Finding adequate space and scheduling acceptable times for all participants

   1.____

2. Assume that, as a manager, you have decided to start a job enrichment program with the purpose of making jobs more varied and interesting in an effort to increase the motivation of a certain group of workers in your division.
   Which one of the following should generally NOT be part of this program?
   A. Increasing the accountability of these individuals for their own work
   B. Granting additional authority or job freedom to these employees in their job activities
   C. Mandating increased monthly production goals for this group of employees
   D. Giving each of these employees a complete unit of work

   2.____

3. Both employer and employee have an important stake in effective preparation for retirement.
   According to modern management thinking, the one of the following which is probably the MOST important aspect of a sound pre-retirement program is to
   A. make assignments that utilize the employee's abilities fully
   B. reassign the employee to a less demanding position in the organization for the last year or two he is on the job
   C. provide the employee with financial data and other facts that would be pertinent to his retirement planning
   D. encourage the employee to develop interests and hobbies which are connected with the job

   3.____

4. The civil service system generally emphasizes a policy of *promotion-from-within*. Employees in the direct line of promotion in a given occupational group are eligible for promotion to the next higher title in that occupational group.
   Which one of the following is LEAST likely to occur as a result of this policy and practice?
   A. Training time will be saved since employees in higher-level positions are already familiar with many agency rules, regulations, and procedures.
   B. The recruitment section will be able to show prospective employees that there are distinct promotional opportunities.

   4.____

48

C. Employees will be provided with a clear-cut picture as to their possible career ladder.
D. Employees will be encouraged to seek broad-based training and education to enhance their promotability.

5. From a management point of view, the MAIAN drawback of seniority as opposed to merit as a basis for granting pay increases to workers is that a pay increase system based on seniority
   A. is favored by unions
   B. upsets organizational status relationships
   C. may encourage mediocre performance by employees
   D. is more difficult to administer than a merit plan

6. One of the actions that is often taken against employees in the non-uniformed forces who are accused of misconduct on the job is suspension without pay. The MOST justifiable reason for taking such action is to
   A. ease an employee out of the agency
   B. enable an investigation to be conducted into the circumstances of the offense
   C. improve the performance of the employee when he returns to the job
   D. punish the employee by imposing a hardship on him

7. A manager has had difficulty in getting good clerical employees to staff a filing section under his supervision. To add to his problems, one of his most competent senior clerks requests a transfer to the accounting division so that he can utilize his new accounting skill, which he is acquiring by going to college at night. The manager attempts to keep the senior clerk in his filing section by calling the director of personnel and getting him to promise not to authorize any transfer.
GENERALLY, this manager's action is
   A. *desirable*; he should not help his staff to develop themselves if it means losing good people
   B. *undesirable*; he should recommend that the senior clerk get a raise in the hope of preventing him from transferring to another section
   C. *desirable*; it shows that the manager is concerned about the senior clerk's future performance
   D. *undesirable*; it is good policy to transfer employees to the type of work they are interested in and for which they are acquiring training

8. One of your subordinates, a unit supervisor, comes to you, the division chief, because he feels that he is working out of title, and he suggests that his competitive class position should be reclassified to a higher title.
Which one of the following statements that the subordinate has made is generally LEAST likely to be a valid support for his suggestion?
   A. The work he is doing conforms to the general statement of duties and responsibilities as described in the class specification for the next higher title in his occupational group.
   B. Most of the typical tasks he performs are listed in the class specification for a title with a higher salary range and are not listed for his current title.

C. His education and experience qualifications far exceed the minimum requirements for the position he holds.
D. His duties and responsibilities have changed recently and are now similar to those of his supervisor.

9. Assume that a class specification for a competitive title used exclusively by your agency is outdated, and that no examination for the title has been given since the specification was issued.
   Of the following, the MOST appropriate action for your agency to take is to
   A. make the necessary changes and submit the revised class specification to the city civil service commission
   B. write the personnel director to recommend that the class specification be updated, giving the reasons and suggested revisions
   C. prepare a revised class specification and submit it to the office of management and budget for their approval
   D. secure approval of the state civil service commission to update the class specification, and then submit the revised specification to the city civil service commission

9.____

10. Assume that an appropriate eligible list has been established and certified to your agency for a title in which a large number of provisionals are serving in your agency.
    In order to obtain permission from the personnel director to retain some of them beyond the usual time limit set by rules (two months) following certification of the list, which one of the following conditions MUST apply?
    A. The positions are sensitive and require investigation of eligibles prior to appointment.
    B. Replacement of all provisionals within two months would impair essential public service.
    C. Employees are required to work rotating shifts, including nights and weekends.
    D. The duties of the positions require unusual physical effort and endurance.

10.____

11. Under the federally-funded Comprehensive Employment and Training Act (CETA), the hiring by the city of non-civil servants for CETA jobs is PROHIBITED when the
    A. applicants are unemployed because of seasonal lay-offs in private industry
    B. applicants do not meet U.S. citizenship and city residence requirements
    C. jobs have minimum requirements of specialized professional or technical training and experience
    D. jobs are comparable to those performed by laid-off civil servants

11.____

12. Assume you are in charge of the duplicating service in your agency. Since employees assigned to this operation lack a sense of accomplishment because the work is highly specialized and repetitive, your superior proposes to enlarge the jobs of these workers and asks you about your reaction to this strategy.

12.____

The MOST appropriate response for you to make is that job enlargement would be
- A. *undesirable*, primarily because it would increase production costs
- B. *undesirable*, primarily because it would diminish the quality of the output
- C. *desirable*, primarily because it might make it possible to add an entire level of management to the organizational structure of your agency
- D. *desirable*, primarily because it might make it possible to decrease the amount of supervision the workers will require

13. According to civil service law, layoff or demotion must be made in inverse order of seniority among employees permanently serving in the same title and layoff unit.
    Which one of the following is now the CORRECT formula for computing seniority?
    Total continuous service in the
    - A. competitive class only
    - B. competitive, non-competitive, or labor class
    - C. classified or unclassified services
    - D. competitive, non-competitive, exempt, and labor classes

14. Under which of the following conditions would an appointing officer be permitted to consider the sex of a candidate in making an employment decision?
    When
    - A. the duties of the position require considerable physical effort or strength
    - B. the duties of the position are considered inherently dangerous
    - C. separate toilet facilities and dressing rooms for the sexes are unavailable and/or cannot be provided in any event
    - D. the public has indicated a preference to be served by persons of a specified sex

15. Assume that an accountant under your supervision signs out to the field to make an agency audit. It is later discovered that, although he had reported himself at work until 5 P.M. that day, he had actually left for home at 3:30 P.M. Although this accountant has worked for the city for ten years and has had an excellent performance record, he is demoted to a lower title in punishment for this breach of duty.
    According to generally accepted thinking on personnel management, the disciplinary action taken in this case should be considered
    - A. *appropriate*; a lesser penalty might encourage repetition of the offense
    - B. *inappropriate*; the correct penalty for such a breach of duty should be dismissal
    - C. *appropriate*; the accountant's abilities may be utilized better in the new assignment
    - D. *inappropriate*; the impact of a continuing stigma and loss of salary is not commensurate with the offense committed

16. Line managers often request more funds for their units than are actually required to attain their current objectives.
Which one of the following is the MOST important reason for such inflated budget requests?
The
   A. expectation that budget examiners will exercise their prerogative of budget cutting
   B. line manager's interest in improving the performance of his unit is thereby indicated to top management
   C. expectation that such requests will make it easier to obtain additional funds in future years
   D. opinion that it makes sense to obtain additional funds and decide later how to use them

17. Integrating budgeting with program planning and evaluation in a city agency is GENERALLY considered to be
   A. *undesirable*; budgeting must focus on the fiscal year at hand, whereas planning must concern itself with developments over a period of years
   B. *desirable*; budgeting facilitates the choice-making process by evaluating the financial implications of agency programs and forcing cost comparisons among them
   C. *undesirable*; accountants and statisticians with the required budgetary skills have little familiarity with the substantive programs that the agency is conducting
   D. *desirable*; such a partnership increases the budgetary skills of planners, thus promoting more effective use of public resources

18. An aspect of the managerial function, a budget is described BEST as a
   A. set of qualitative management controls over productivity
   B. tool based on historical accounting reports
   C. type of management plan expressed in quantitative terms
   D. precise estimate of future quantitative and qualitative contingencies

19. Which one of the following is generally accepted as the MAJOR immediate advantage of installing a system of program budgeting?
It
   A. encourages managers to relate their decisions to the agency's long-range goals
   B. is a replacement for the financial or fiscal budget
   C. decreases the need for managers to make trade-offs in the decision-making process
   D. helps to adjust budget figures to provide for unexpected developments

20. Of the following, the BEST means for assuring necessary responsiveness of a budgetary program to changing conditions is by
   A. overestimating budgetary expenditures by 15% and assigning the excess to unforeseen problem areas
   B. underestimating budgetary expenditures by at least 20% and setting aside a reserve account in the same amount

C. reviewing and revising the budget at regular intervals so that it retains its character as a current document
D. establishing *budget-by-exception* policies for each division in the agency

21. According to expert thought in the area of budgeting, participation in the preparation of a government agency's budget should GENERALLY involve
    A. only top management
    B. only lower levels of management
    C. all levels of the organization
    D. only a central budget office or bureau

22. Of the following, the MOST useful guide to analysis of budget estimates for the coming fiscal year is a comparison with
    A. appropriations as amended for the current fiscal year
    B. manpower requirements for the previous two years
    C. initial appropriations for the current fiscal year
    D. budget estimates for the preceding five years

23. A manager assigned to analyze the costs and benefits associated with a program which the agency head proposes to undertake may encounter certain factors which cannot be measured in dollar terms.
    In such a case, the manager should GENERALLY
    A. ignore the factors which cannot be quantified
    B. evaluate the factors in accordance with their degree of importance to the overall agency goals
    C. give the factors weight equal to the weight given to measurable costs and benefits
    D. assume that non-measurable costs and benefits will balance out against one another

24. If city employees believe that they are receiving adverse treatment in terms of training and disciplinary actions because of their national origin, they may file charges of discrimination with the Federal government's
    A. Human Rights Commission
    B. Public Employee Relations Board
    C. Equal Employment Opportunity Commission
    D. United States Department of Commerce

25. Under existing employment statutes, the city is obligated, as an employer, to take *affirmative action* in certain instances.
    This requirement has been imposed to ensure that
    A. employees who are members of minority groups, or women, be given special opportunities for training and promotion even though they are not available to other employees
    B. employees or applicants for employment are treated without regard to race, color, religion, sex, or national origin

C. proof exists to show that the city has acted with good intentions in any case where it has disregarded this requirement
D. men and women are treated alike except where State law provides special hour or working conditions for women

KEY (CORRECT ANSWERS)

1. B
2. C
3. C
4. D
5. C

6. B
7. D
8. C
9. B
10. B

11. D
12. D
13. D
14. C
15. D

16. A
17. B
18. C
19. A
20. D

21. C
22. A
23. B
24. C
25. B

EXAMINATION SECTION
TEST 1

DIRECTIONS: Each question or incomplete statement is followed by several suggested answers or completions. Select the one that BEST answers the question or completes the statement. *PRINT THE LETTER OF THE CORRECT ANSWER IN THE SPACE AT THE RIGHT.*

1. Assume that a manager is preparing a list of reasons to justify making a major change in methods and procedures in his agency.
   Which of the following reasons would be LEAST appropriate on such a list?
   A. Improve the means for satisfying needs and wants of agency personnel
   B. Increase efficiency
   C. Intensify competition and stimulate loyalty to separate work groups
   D. Contribute to the individual and group satisfaction of agency personnel

   1.____

2. Many managers recognize the benefits of decentralization but are concerned about the danger of over-relaxation of control as a result of increased delegation.
   Of the following, the MOST appropriate means of establishing proper control under decentralization is for the manager to
   A. establish detailed standards for all phases of operation
   B. shift his attention from operating details to appraisal of results
   C. keep himself informed by decreasing the time span covered by reports
   D. make unilateral decisions on difficult situations that arise in decentralized locations

   2.____

3. In some agencies, the counsel to the agency head is given the right to bypass the chain of command and issue orders directly to the staff concerning matters that involve certain specific processes and practices.
   This situation MOST NEARLY illustrates the principle of _____ authority.
   A. the acceptance theory of   B. multiple-linear
   C. splintered   D. functional

   3.____

4. Assume that a manager is writing a brief report to his superior outlining the advantages of matrix organization.
   Of the following, it would be INCORRECT to state that
   A. in matrix organization, a project is emphasized by designating one individual as the focal point for all matters pertaining to it
   B. utilization of manpower can be flexible in matrix organization because a reservoir of specialists is maintained in the line operations
   C. the usual line staff arrangement is generally reversed in matrix organization
   D. in matrix organization, responsiveness to project needs is generally faster due to establishing needed communication lines and decision points

   4.____

5. It is commonly understood that communication is an important part of the administrative process.
Which of the following is NOT a valid principle of the communication process in administration?
   A. The channels of communication should be spontaneous.
   B. The lines of communication should be as direct and as short as possible.
   C. Communications should be authenticated.
   D. The persons serving in communications centers should be competent.

6. The PRIMARY purpose of the quantitative approach in management is to
   A. identify better alternatives for management decision-making
   B. substitute data for judgment
   C. match opinions to data
   D. match data to opinions

7. If an executive wants to make a strong case for running his agency as a flat type of structure, he should point out that the PRIMARY advantage of doing so is to
   A. provide less experience in decision-making for agency personnel
   B. facilitate frequent contact between each superior and his immediate subordinates
   C. improve communication and unify attitudes
   D. improve communication and diversify attitudes

8. In deciding how detailed his delegation of authority to a subordinate should be, a manager should follow the general principle that
   A. delegation of authority is more detailed at the top of the organizational structure
   B. detailed delegation of authority is associated with detailed work assignments
   C. delegation of authority should be in sufficient detail to prevent overlapping assignments
   D. detailed delegation of authority is associated with broad work assignments

9. In recent years, newer and more fluid types of organizational forms have been developed. One of these is a type of free-form organization.
Another name for this type of organization is the
   A. project organization   B. semimix organization
   C. naturalistic structure   D. semipermanent structure

10. Which of the following is the MAJOR objective of operational or management systems audits?
    A. Determining the number of personnel needed
    B. Recommending opportunities for improving operating and management practices
    C. Detecting fraud
    D. Determining organization problems

11. Assume that a manager observes that conflict exists between his agency and another operating agency of government.
    Which of the following statements is the LEAST probable cause of this conflict?
    A. Incompatibility between the agencies' goals but similarity in their resource allocations
    B. Compatibility between agencies' goals and resources
    C. Status differences between agency personnel
    D. Differences in perceptions of each other's policies

12. Of the following, a MAJOR purpose of brainstorming as a problem-solving technique is to
    A. develop the ability to concentrate
    B. encourage creative thinking
    C. evaluate employees' ideas
    D. develop critical ability

13. The one of the following requirements which is LEAST likely to accompany regular delegation of work from a manager to a subordinate is a(n)
    A. need to review the organization's workload
    B. indication of what work the subordinate is to do
    C. need to grant authority to the subordinate
    D. obligation for the subordinate who accepts the work to try to complete it

14. Of the following, the one factor which is generally considered LEAST essential to successful committee operation is
    A. stating a clear definition of the authority and scope of the committee
    B. selecting the committee chairman carefully
    C. limiting the size of the committee to four persons
    D. limiting the subject matter to that which can be handled in group discussion

15. In using the program evaluation and review technique, the *critical path* is the path that
    A. requires the shortest time
    B. requires the longest time
    C. focuses most attention on social constraints
    D. focuses most attention to repetitious jobs

16. Which one of the following is LEAST characteristic of the management-by-objectives approach?
    A. The scope within which the employee may exercise decision-making is broadened.
    B. The employee starts with a self-appraisal of his performances, abilities, and potential.
    C. Emphasis is placed on activities performed; activities orientation is maximized.
    D. Each employee participates in determining his own objectives.

17. The function of management which puts into effect the decisions, plans, and programs that have previously been worked out for achieving the goals of the group is MOST appropriately called
    A. scheduling   B. classifying   C. budgeting   D. directing

18. In the establishment of a plan to improve office productive efficiency, which of the following guidelines is LEAST helpful in setting sound work standards?
    A. Employees must accept the plan's objectives.
    B. Current production averages must be promulgated as work standards for a group.
    C. The work flow must generally be fairly constant.
    D. The operation of the plan must be expressed in terms understandable to the worker.

19. The one of the following activities which, generally speaking, is of *relatively* MAJOR importance at the lower-management level and of *somewhat* LESSER importance at higher-management levels is
    A. actuating   B. forecasting   C. organizing   D. planning

20. Three styles of leadership exist: democratic, authoritarian, and laissez-faire. Of the following work situations, the one in which a democratic approach would normally be the MOST effective is when the work is
    A. routine and moderately complex   B. repetitious and simple
    C. complex and not routine   D. simple and not routine

21. Governmental and business organizations *generally* encounter the GREATEST difficulties in developing tangible measures of which one of the following?
    A. The level of expenditures   B. Contributions to social welfare
    C. Retention rates   D. Causes of labor unrest

22. Of the following, a *management-by-objectives* program is BEST described as
    A. a new comprehensive plan of organization
    B. introduction of budgets and financial controls
    C. introduction of long-range planning
    D. development of future goals with supporting and related progress reviews

23. Research and analysis is probably the most widely used technique for selecting alternatives when major planning decisions are involved.
    Of the following, a VALUABLE characteristic of research and analysis is that this technique
    A. places the problem in a meaningful conceptual framework
    B. involves practical application of the various alternatives
    C. accurately analyzes all important tangibles
    D. is much less expensive than other problem-solving methods

24. If a manager were assigned the task of using a systems approach to designing a new work unit, which of the following should he consider FIRST in carrying out his design?
    A. Networks
    B. Work flows and information processes
    C. Linkages and relationships
    D. Decision points and control loops

25. The MAIN distinction between Theory X and Theory Y approaches to organization, in accordance with Douglas McGregor's view, is that Theory Y
    A. considers that work is natural to people; Theory X assumes that people are lazy and avoid work
    B. leads to a tall, narrow organization structure, while Theory X leads to one that is flat
    C. organizations motivate people with money; Theory X organizations motivate people with good working conditions
    D. represents authoritarian management, while Theory X management is participative

KEY (CORRECT ANSWERS)

1.	C	11.	B
2.	B	12.	B
3.	D	13.	A
4.	C	14.	C
5.	A	15.	B
6.	A	16.	C
7.	C	17.	D
8.	B	18.	B
9.	A	19.	A
10.	B	20.	C

21.	B
22.	D
23.	A
24.	B
25.	A

TEST 2

DIRECTIONS: Each question or incomplete statement is followed by several suggested answers or completions. Select the one that BEST answers the question or completes the statement. *PRINT THE LETTER OF THE CORRECT ANSWER IN THE SPACE AT THE RIGHT.*

1. Of the following, the stage in decision-making which is usually MOST difficult is
   A. stating the alternatives
   B. predicting the possible outcome of each alternative
   C. evaluating the relative merits of each alternative
   D. minimizing the undesirable aspects of the alternative selected

   1.____

2. In a department where a clerk is reporting both to a senior clerk in charge of the mail room and also to a supervising clerk in charge of the duplicating section, there may be a breakdown of the management principle called
   A. horizontal specialization   B. job enrichment
   C. unity of command   D. Graicunas' Law

   2.____

3. Of the following, the failure by line managers to accept and appreciate the benefits and limitations of a new program or system VERY frequently can be traced to the
   A. budgetary problems involved
   B. resultant need to reduce staff
   C. lack of controls it engenders
   D. failure of top management to support its implementation

   3.____

4. Although there is general agreement that *management-by-objectives* has made a major contribution to modern management of large organizations, criticisms of the system during the past few years have resulted in
   A. mounting pressure for relaxation of management goals
   B. renewed concern with human values and the manager's personal needs
   C. over-mechanistic application of the perceptions of the behavioral scientists
   D. disillusionment with *management-by-objectives* on the part of a majority of managers

   4.____

5. Of the following, which is usually considered to be a MAJOR obstacle to the systematic analysis of potential problems by managers?
   A. Managers have a tendency to think that all the implications of some proposed step cannot be fully understood.
   B. Rewards rarely go to those managers who are most successful at resolving current problems in management.
   C. There is a common conviction of manages that their goals are difficult to achieve.
   D. Managers are far more concerned about correcting today's problems than with preventing tomorrow's.

   5.____

6. Which of the following should generally have the MOST influence on the selection of supervisors?
   A. Experience within the work unit where the vacancies exist
   B. Amount of money needed to effect the promotion
   C. Personal preferences of the administration
   D. Evaluation of capacity to exercise supervisory responsibilities

7. In questioning a potential administrator for selection purposes, the one of the following practices which is MOST desirable is to
   A. encourage the job applicant to give primarily *yes* or *no* replies
   B. get the applicant to talk freely and in detail about his background
   C. let the job applicant speak most of the time
   D. probe the applicant's attitudes, motivation, and willingness to accept responsibility

8. In implementing the managerial function of training subordinates, it is USEFUL to know that a widely agreed-upon definition of human learning is that learning
   A. is a relatively permanent change in behavior that results from reinforced practice or experience
   B. involves an improvement, but not necessarily a change in behavior
   C. involves a change in behavior, but not necessarily an improvement
   D. is a temporary change in behavior which must be subject to practice or experience

9. If a manager were thinking about using a committee of subordinates to solve an operating problem, which of the following would generally NOT be an advantage of such use of the committee approach?
   A. Improved coordination   B. Low cost
   C. Increased motivation   D. Integrated judgment

10. Which one of the following management approaches MOST often uses model-building techniques to solve management problems? _____ approach.
    A. Behavioral   B. Fiscal   C. Quantitative   D. Process

11. Of the following, the MOST serious risk in using budgets as a tool for management control is the
    A. probable neglect of other good management practices
    B. likelihood of guesswork because of the need to plan far in advance
    C. possibility of undue emphasis on factors that are easiest to measure
    D. danger of making qualitative rather than quantitative assessments of performance

12. In government budgeting, the problem of relating financial transactions to the fiscal year in which they are budgeted is BEST met by
    A. determining the cash balance by comparing how much money has been received and how much has been paid out
    B. applying net revenue to the fiscal year in which they are collected as offset by relevant expenses

C. adopting a system whereby appropriations are entered when they are received and expenditures are entered when they are paid out
D. entering expenditures on the books when the obligation to make the expenditure is made

13. If the agency's bookkeeping system records income when it is received and expenditures when the money is paid out this system is USUALLY known as a _____ system.
    A. cash
    B. flow-payment
    C. deferred
    D. fiscal year income

14. An audit, as the term applies to budget execution, is MOST NEARLY a
    A. procedure based on the budget estimates
    B. control exercised by the executive on the legislature in the establishment of program priorities
    C. check on the legality of expenditures and is based on the appropriations act
    D. requirement which must be met before funds can be spent

15. In government budgeting, there is a procedure known as *allotment*.
    Of the following statements which relate to allotment, select the one that is MOST generally considered to be correct.
    Allotment
    A. increases the practice of budget units coming back to the legislature branch for supplemental appropriations
    B. is simply an example of red tape
    C. eliminates the requirement of timing of expenditures
    D. is designed to prevent waste

16. In government budgeting, the establishment of the schedules of allotments is MOST generally the responsibility of the
    A. budget unit and the legislature
    B. budget unit and the executive
    C. budget unit only
    D. executive and the legislature

17. Of the following statements relating to preparation of an organization's budget request, which is the MOST generally valid precaution?
    A. Give specific instructions on the format or budget requests and required supporting data
    B. Because of the complexity of preparing a budget request, avoid argumentation to support the requests
    C. Put requests in whatever format is desirable
    D. Consider that final approval will be given to initial estimates

18. Of the following statements which relate to the budget process in a well-organized government, select the one that is MOST NEARLY correct.
    A. The budget cycle is the step-by-step process which is repeated each and every fiscal year.
    B. Securing approval of the budget does not take place within the budget cycle.

C. The development of a new budget and putting it into effect is a two-step process known as the budget cycle.
D. The fiscal period, usually a fiscal year, has no relation to the budget cycle.

19. If a manager were asked what PPBS stands for, he would be RIGHT if he said _____ budgeting system.
    A. public planning
    B. planning programming
    C. planning projections
    D. programming procedures

19._____

Questions 20-21.

DIRECTIONS: Questions 20 and 21 are to be answered on the basis of the following information.

Sample Budget

Refuse Collection	Amount
Personal Services	$30,000
Contractual Services	5,000
Supplies and Materials	5,000
Capital Outlay	10,000
	$50,000

Residential Collections	
Dwellings – 1 pickup per week	1,000
Tons of refuse collected per year	375
Cost of collections per ton	$ 8
Cost per dwelling pickup per year	$ 3
Total annual cost	$3,000

20. The sample budget shown is a simplified example of a _____ budget.
    A. factorial   B. performance   C. qualitative   D. rational

20._____

21. The budget shown in the sample differs CHIEFLY from line-item and program budgets in that it includes
    A. objects of expenditure but not activities or functions
    B. only activities, functions, and control
    C. activities and functions but not objects of expenditures
    D. levels of service

21._____

Question 22.

DIRECTIONS: Question 22 is to be answered on the basis of the following information.

Sample Budget

Environmental Safety
  Air Pollution Protection
    Personal Services $20,000,000
    Contractual Services   4,000,000
    Supplies and Materials   4,000,000
    Capital Outlay   2,000,000
      Total Air Pollution Protection $30,000,000

  Water Pollution Protection
    Personal Services $23,000,000
    Supplies and Materials   4,500,000
    Capital Outlay   20,500,000
      Total Water Pollution Protection $48,000,000

Total Environmental Safety $78,000,000

22. Based on the above budget, which is the MOST valid statement?
    A. Environmental Safety, Air Pollution Protection, and Water Pollution Protection could all be considered program elements.
    B. The object listings included water pollution protection and capital outlay.
    C. Examples of the program element listings in the above are personal services and supplies and materials
    D. Contractual Services and Environmental Safety were the program element listings.

23. Which of the following is NOT an advantage of a program budget over a line-item budget?
    A program budget
    A. allows us to set up priority lists in deciding what activities we will spend our money on
    B. gives us more control over expenditures than a line-item budget
    C. is more informative in that we know the broad purposes of spending money
    D. enables us to see if one program is getting much less money than the others

24. If a manager were trying to explain the fundamental difference between traditional accounting theory and practice and the newer practice of managerial accounting, he would be MOST accurate if he said that
    A. traditional accounting practice focused on providing information for persons outside organizations, while managerial accounting focuses on providing information for people inside organizations
    B. traditional accounting practice focused on providing information for persons inside organizations while managerial accounting focuses on providing information for persons outside organizations

C. managerial accounting is exclusively concerned with historical facts while traditional accounting stresses future projections exclusively
D. traditional accounting practice is more budget-focused than managerial accounting

25. Which of the following formulas is used to determine the number of days required to process work?
_____ = Days to Process Work

A. $\dfrac{\text{Employees} \times \text{Daily Output}}{\text{Volume}}$

B. $\dfrac{\text{Volume} \times \text{Daily Output}}{\text{Volume}}$

C. $\dfrac{\text{Volume}}{\text{Employees} \times \text{Daily Output}}$

D. $\dfrac{\text{Employees} \times \text{Volume}}{\text{Daily Output}}$

25.____

KEY (CORRECT ANSWERS)

1.	C	11.	C
2.	C	12.	D
3.	D	13.	A
4.	B	14.	C
5.	D	15.	D
6.	D	16.	C
7.	D	17.	A
8.	A	18.	A
9.	B	19.	B
10.	C	20.	B

21. D
22. A
23. B
24. A
25. C

TEST 3

DIRECTIONS: Each question or incomplete statement is followed by several suggested answers or completions. Select the one that BEST answers the question or completes the statement. *PRINT THE LETTER OF THE CORRECT ANSWER IN THE SPACE AT THE RIGHT.*

1. Electronic data processing equipment can produce more information faster than can be generated by any other means.
   In view of this, the MOST important problem faced by management at present is to
   A. keep computers fully occupied
   B. find enough computer personnel
   C. assimilate and properly evaluate the information
   D. obtain funds to establish appropriate information systems

   1.____

2. A well-designed management information system ESSENTIALLY provides each executive and manager the information he needs for
   A. determining computer time requirements
   B. planning and measuring results
   C. drawing a new organization chart
   D. developing a new office layout

   2.____

3. It is generally agreed that management policies should be periodically reappraised and restated in accordance with current conditions.
   Of the following, the approach which would be MOST effective in determining whether a policy should be revised is to
   A. conduct interviews with staff members at all levels in order to ascertain the relationship between the policy and actual practice
   B. make proposed revisions in the policy and apply it to current problems
   C. make up hypothetical situations using both the old policy and a revised version in order to make comparisons
   D. call a meeting of top level staff in order to discuss ways of revising the policy

   3.____

4. Every manager has many occasions to lead a conference or participate in a conference of some sort.
   Of the following statements that pertain to conferences and conference leadership, which is generally considered to be MOST valid?
   A. Since World War II, the trend has been toward fewer shared decisions and more conferences.
   B. The most important part of a conference leader's job is to direct discussion.
   C. In providing opportunities for group interaction, management should avoid consideration of its past management philosophy.
   D. A good administrator cannot lead a good conference if he is a poor public speaker.

   4.____

5. Of the following, it is usually LEAST desirable for a conference leader to
   A. turn the question to the person who asked it
   B. summarize proceedings periodically
   C. make a practice of not repeating questions
   D. ask a question without indicating who is to reply

6. The behavioral school of management thought bases its beliefs on certain assumptions.
   Which of the following is NOT a belief of this school of thought?
   A. People tend to seek and accept responsibility.
   B. Most people can be creative in solving problems.
   C. People prefer security above all else.
   D. Commitment is the most important factor in motivating people.

7. The one of the following objectives which would be LEAST appropriate as a major goal of research in the field of human resources management is to
   A. predict future conditions, events, and manpower needs
   B. evaluate established policies, programs, and practices
   C. evaluate proposed policies, programs, and practices
   D. identify deficient organizational units and apply suitable penalties

8. Of the following general interviewing methods or techniques, the one that is USUALLY considered to be effective in counseling, grievances, and appraisal interviews is the _____ interview.
   A. directed   B. non-directed   C. panel   D. patterned

9. The ESSENTIAL first phase of decision-making is
   A. finding alternative solutions
   B. making a diagnosis of the problem
   C. selecting the plan to follow
   D. analyzing and comparing alternative solutions

10. Assume that, in a certain organization, a situation has developed in which there is little difference in status or authority between individuals.
    Which of the following would be the MOST likely result with regard to communication in this organization?
    A. Both the accuracy and flow of communication will be improved.
    B. Both the accuracy and flow of communication will substantially decrease.
    C. Employees will seek more formal lines of communication.
    D. Neither the flow nor the accuracy of communication will be improved over the former hierarchical structure.

11. The main function of many agency administrative offices is *information management*. Information that is received by an administrative officer may be classified as active or passive, depending upon whether or not it requires the recipient to take some action.

Of the following, the item received which is clearly the MOST active information is
- A. an appointment of a new staff member
- B. a payment voucher for a new desk
- C. a press release concerning a past city event
- D. the minutes of a staff meeting

12. Which one of the following sets BEST describes the general order in which to teach an operation to a new employee?
    - A. Prepare, present, tryout, follow-up
    - B. Prepare, test, tryout, re-test
    - C. Present, test, tryout, follow-up
    - D. Test, present, follow-up, re-test

13. Of the following, public employees may be separated from public service
    - A. for the same reasons which are generally acceptable for discharging employees in private industry
    - B. only under the most trying circumstances
    - C. under procedures that are neither formalized nor subject to review
    - D. solely in extreme cases involving offenses of gravest character

14. Of the following, the one LEAST considered to be a communication barrier is
    - A. group feedback
    - B. charged words
    - C. selective perception
    - D. symbolic meanings

15. Of the following ways for a manager to handle his appointments, the BEST way, according to experts in administration, generally is to
    - A. schedule his own appointments and inform his secretary not to reserve his time without his approval
    - B. encourage everyone to make appointments through his secretary and tell her when he makes his own appointments
    - C. see no one who has not made a previous appointment
    - D. permit anyone to see him without an appointment

16. Assume that a manager decides to examine closely one of five units under his supervision to uncover problems common to all five.
    His research technique is MOST closely related to the method called
    - A. experimentation
    - B. simulation
    - C. linear analysis
    - D. sampling

17. If one views the process of management as a dynamic process, which one of the following functions is NOT a legitimate part of that process?
    - A. Communication
    - B. Decision-making
    - C. Organizational slack
    - D. Motivation

18. Which of the following would be the BEST statement of a budget-oriented purpose for a government administrator? To
    A. provide 200 hours of instruction in basic reading for 3,500 adult illiterates at a cost of $1 million in the next fiscal year
    B. inform the public of adult educational programs
    C. facilitate the transfer to a city agency of certain functions of a federally-funded program which is being phased out
    D. improve the reading skills of the adult citizens in the city

19. Modern management philosophy and practices are changing to accommodate the expectations and motivations of organization personnel.
    Which of the following terms INCORRECTLY describes these newer managerial approaches?
    A. Rational management
    B. Participative management
    C. Decentralization
    D. Democratic supervision

20. Management studies support the hypothesis that, in spite of the tendency of employees to censor the information communicated to their supervisor, subordinates are MORE likely to communicate problem-oriented information upward when they have
    A. a long period of service in the organization
    B. a high degree of trust in the supervisor
    C. a high educational level
    D. low status on the organizational ladder

KEY (CORRECT ANSWERS)

1.	C	11.	A
2.	B	12.	A
3.	A	13.	A
4.	B	14.	A
5.	A	15.	B
6.	C	16.	D
7.	D	17.	C
8.	B	18.	A
9.	B	19.	A
10.	D	20.	B

COMMUNICATION
EXAMINATION SECTION
TEST 1

DIRECTIONS: Each question or incomplete statement is followed by several suggested answers or completions. Select the one that BEST answers the question or completes the statement. *PRINT THE LETTER OF THE CORRECT ANSWER IN THE SPACE AT THE RIGHT.*

1. In some agencies the counsel to the agency head is given the right to bypass the chain of command and issue orders directly to the staff concerning matters that involve certain specific processes and practices.
   This situation MOST nearly illustrates the principle of _____ authority.
   A. the acceptance theory of
   B. multiple-linear
   C. splintered
   D. functional

   1.____

2. It is commonly understood that communication is an important part of the administrative process.
   Which of the following is NOT a valid principle of the communication process in administration?
   A. The channels of communication should be spontaneous.
   B. The lines of communication should be as direct and as short as possible.
   C. Communications should be authenticated.
   D. The persons serving in communications centers should be competent.

   2.____

3. Of the following, the one factor which is generally considered LEAST essential to successful committee operations is
   A. stating a clear definition of the authority and scope of the committee
   B. selecting the committee chairman carefully
   C. limiting the size of the committee to four persons
   D. limiting the subject matter to that which can be handled in group discussion

   3.____

4. Of the following, the failure by line managers to accept and appreciate the benefits and limitations of a new program or system VERY FREQUENTLY can be traced to the
   A. budgetary problems involved
   B. resultant need to reduce staff
   C. lack of controls it engenders
   D. failure of top management to support its implementation

   4.____

5. If a manager were thinking about using a committee of subordinates to solve an operating problem, which of the following would generally NOT be an advantage of such use of the committee approach?
   A. Improved coordination
   B. Low cost
   C. Increased motivation
   D. Integrated judgment

   5.____

6. Every supervisor has many occasions to lead a conference or participate in a conference of some sort.
Of the following statements that pertain to conferences and conference leadership, which is generally considered to be MOST valid?
   A. Since World War II, the trend has been toward fewer shared decisions and more conferences.
   B. The most important part of a conference leader's job is to direct discussion.
   C. In providing opportunities for group interaction, management should avoid consideration of its past management philosophy.
   D. A good administrator cannot lead a good conference if he is a poor public speaker.

7. Of the following, it is usually LEAST desirable for a conference leader to
   A. call the name of a person after asking a question
   B. summarize proceedings periodically
   C. make a practice of repeating questions
   D. ask a question without indicating who is to reply

8. Assume that, in a certain organization, a situation has developed in which there is little difference in status or authority between individuals.
Which of the following would be the MOST likely result with regard to communication in this organization?
   A. Both the accuracy and flow of communication will be improved.
   B. Both the accuracy and flow of communication will substantially decrease.
   C. Employees will seek more formal lines of communication.
   D. Neither the flow nor the accuracy of communication will be improved over the former hierarchical structure.

9. The main function of many agency administrative officers is "information management." Information that is received by an administrative officer may be classified as active or passive, depending upon whether or not it requires the recipient to take some action.
Of the following, the item received which is clearly the MOST active information is
   A. an appointment of a new staff member
   B. a payment voucher for a new desk
   C. a press release concerning a past event
   D. the minutes of a staff meeting

10. Of the following, the one LEAST considered to be a communication barrier is
    A. group feedback   B. charged words
    C. selective perception D. symbolic meanings

11. Management studies support the hypothesis that, in spite of the tendency of employees to censor the information communicated to their supervisor, subordinates are more likely to communicate problem-oriented information UPWARD when they have a
    A. long period of service in the organization
    B. high degree of trust in the supervisor
    C. high educational level
    D. low status on the organizational ladder

12. Electronic data processing equipment can produce more information faster than can be generated by any other means.
    In view of this, the MOST important problem faced by management at present is to
    A. keep computers fully occupied
    B. find enough computer personnel
    C. assimilate and properly evaluate the information
    D. obtain funds to establish appropriate information systems

13. A well-designed management information system essentially provides each executive and manager the information he needs for
    A. determining computer time requirements
    B. planning and measuring results
    C. drawing a new organization chart
    D. developing a new office layout

14. It is generally agreed that management policies should be periodically reappraised and restated in accordance with current conditions.
    Of the following, the approach which would be MOST effective in determining whether a policy should be revised is to
    A. conduct interviews with staff members at all levels in order to ascertain the relationship between the policy and actual practice
    B. make proposed revisions in the policy and apply it to current problems
    C. make up hypothetical situations using both the old policy and a revised version in order to make comparisons
    D. call a meeting of top level staff in order to discuss ways of revising the policy

15. Your superior has asked you to notify division employees of an important change in one of the operating procedures described in the division manual. Every employee presently has a copy of this manual.
    Which of the following is normally the MOST practical way to get the employees to understand such a change?
    A. Notify each employee individually of the change and answer any questions he might have
    B. Send a written notice to key personnel, directing them to inform the people under them

C. Call a general meeting, distribute a corrected page for the manual, and discuss the change
D. Send a memo to employees describing the change in general terms and asking them to make the necessary corrections in their copies of the manual

16. Assume that the work in your department involves the use of any technical terms.
    In such a situation, when you are answering inquiries from the general public, it would usually be BEST to
    A. use simple language and avoid the technical terms
    B. employ the technical terms whenever possible
    C. bandy technical terms freely, but explain each term in parentheses
    D. apologize if you are forced to use a technical term

17. Suppose that you receive a telephone call from someone identifying himself as an employee in another city department who asks to be given information which your own department regards as confidential.
    Which of the following is the BEST way of handling such a request?
    A. Give the information requested, since your caller as official standing
    B. Grant the request, provided the caller gives you a signed receipt
    C. Refuse the request, because you have no way of knowing whether the caller is really who he claims to be
    D. Explain that the information is confidential and inform the caller of the channels he must go through to have the information released to him

18. Studies show that office employees place high importance on the social and human aspects of the organization. What office employees like best about their jobs is the kind of people with whom they work. So strive hard to group people who are most likely to get along well together.
    Based on this information, it is MOST reasonable to assume that office workers are most pleased to work in a group which
    A. is congenial   B. has high productivity
    C. allows individual creativity D. is unlike other groups

19. A certain supervisor does not compliment members of his staff when they come up with good ideas. He feels that coming up with good ideas is part of the job and does not merit special attention.
    This supervisor's practice is
    A. *poor*, because recognition for good ideas is a good motivator
    B. *poor*, because the staff will suspect that the supervisor has no good ideas of his own
    C. *good*, because it is reasonable to assume that employees will tell their supervisor of ways to improve office practice
    D. *good*, because the other members of the staff are not made to seem inferior by comparison

5 (#1)

20. Some employees of a department have sent an anonymous letter containing many complaints to the department head.
Of the following, what is this MOST likely to show about the department?
    A. It is probably a good place to work.
    B. Communications are probably poor.
    C. The complaints are probably unjustified.
    D. These employees are probably untrustworthy.

20.____

21. Which of the following actions would usually be MOST appropriate for a supervisor to take after receiving an instruction sheet from his superior explaining a new procedure which is to be followed?
    A. Put the instruction sheet aside temporarily until he determines what is wrong with the old procedure.
    B. Call his superior and ask whether the procedure is one he must implement immediately.
    C. Write a memorandum to the superior asking for more details.
    D. Try the new procedure and advise the superior of any problems or possible improvements.

21.____

22. Of the following, which one is considered the PRIMARY advantage of using a committee to resolved a problem in an organization?
    A. No one person will be held accountable for the decision since a group of people was involved.
    B. People with different backgrounds give attention to the problem.
    C. The decision will take considerable time so there is unlikely to be a decision that will later be regretted.
    D. One person cannot dominate the decision-making process.

22.____

23. Employees in a certain office come to their supervisor with all their complaints about the office and the work. Almost every employee has had at least one minor complaint at some time.
The situation with respect to complaints in this office may BEST be described as probably
    A. *good*; employees who complain care about their jobs and work hard
    B. *good*; grievances brought out into the open can be corrected
    C. *bad*; only serious complaints should be discussed
    D. *bad*; it indicates the staff does not have confidence in the administration

23.____

24. The administrator who allows his staff to suggest ways to do their work will usually find that
    A. this practice contributes to high productivity
    B. the administrator's ideas produce greater output
    C. clerical employees suggest inefficient work methods
    D. subordinate employees resent performing a management function

24.____

25. The MAIN purpose for a supervisor's questioning the employees at a conference he is holding is to
    A. stress those areas of information covered but not understood by the participants
    B. encourage participants to think through the problem under discussion
    C. catch those subordinates who are not paying attention
    D. permit the more knowledgeable participants to display their grasp of the problems being discussed

25.____

KEY (CORRECT ANSWERS)

1.	D		11.	B
2.	A		12.	C
3.	C		13.	B
4.	D		14.	A
5.	B		15.	C
6.	B		16.	A
7.	C		17.	D
8.	D		18.	A
9.	A		19.	A
10.	A		20.	B

21. D
22. B
23. B
24. A
25. B

TEST 2

DIRECTIONS: Each question or incomplete statement is followed by several suggested answers or completions. Select the one that BEST answers the question or completes the statement. *PRINT THE LETTER OF THE CORRECT ANSWER IN THE SPACE AT THE RIGHT.*

1. For a superior to use *consultative supervision* with his subordinates effectively, it is ESSENTIAL that he
   A. accept the fact that his formal authority will be weakened by the procedure
   B. admit that he does not know more than all his men together and that his ideas are not always best
   C. utilize a committee system so that the procedure is orderly
   D. make sure that all subordinates are consulted so that no one feels left out

   1.____

2. The *grapevine* is an informal means of communication in an organization. The attitude of a supervisor with respect to the grapevine should be to
   A. ignore it since it deals mainly with rumors and sensational information
   B. regard it as a serious danger which should be eliminated
   C. accept it as a real line of communication which should be listened to
   D. utilize it for most purposes instead of the official line of communication

   2.____

3. The supervisor of an office that must deal with the public should realize that planning in this type of work situation
   A. is useless because he does not know how many people will request service or what service they will request
   B. must be done at a higher level but that he should be ready to implement the results of such planning
   C. is useful primarily for those activities that are not concerned with public contact
   D. is useful for all the activities of the office, including those that relate to public contact

   3.____

4. Assume that it is your job to receive incoming telephone calls. Those calls which you cannot handle yourself have to be transferred to the appropriate office.
   If you receive an outside call for an extension line which is busy, the one of the following which you should do FIRST is to
   A. interrupt the person speaking on the extension and tell him a call is waiting
   B. tell the caller the line is busy and let him know every thirty seconds whether or not it is free
   C. leave the caller on "hold" until the extension is free
   D. tell the caller the line is busy and ask him if he wishes to wait

   4.____

77

5. Your superior has subscribed to several publications directly related to your division's work, and he has asked you to see to it that the publications are circulated among the supervisory personnel in the division. There are eight supervisors involved.
The BEST method of insuring that all eight see these publications is to
   A. place the publication in the division's general reference library as soon as it arrives
   B. inform each supervisor whenever a publication arrives and remind all of them that they are responsible for reading it
   C. prepare a standard slip that can be stapled to each publication, listing the eight supervisors and saying, "Please read, initial your name, and pass along"
   D. send a memo to the eight supervisors saying that they may wish to purchase individual subscriptions in their own names if they are interested in seeing each issue

5.____

6. Your superior has telephoned a number of key officials in your agency to ask whether they can meet at a certain time next month. He has found that they can all make it, and he has asked you to confirm the meeting.
Which of the following is the BEST way to confirm such a meeting?
   A. Note the meeting on your superior's calendar.
   B. Post a notice of the meeting on the agency bulletin board.
   C. Call the officials on the day of the meeting to remind them of the meeting.
   D. Write a memo to each official involved, repeating the time and place of the meeting.

6.____

7. Assume that a new city regulation requires that certain kinds of private organizations file information forms with your department. You have been asked to write the short explanatory message that will be printed on the front cover of the pamphlet containing the forms and instructions.
Which of the following would be the MOST appropriate way of beginning this message?
   A. Get the readers' attention by emphasizing immediately that there are legal penalties for organizations that fail to file before a certain date.
   B. Briefly state the nature of the enclosed forms and the types of organizations that must file.
   C. Say that your department is very sorry to have to put organizations to such an inconvenience.
   D. Quote the entire regulation adopted by the city, even if it is quite long and is expressed din complicated legal language.

7.____

8. Suppose that you have been told to make up the vacation schedule for the 18 employees in a particular unit. In order for the unit to operate effectively, only a few employees can be on vacation at the same time.
Which of the following is the MOST advisable approach in making up the schedule?
   A. Draw up a schedule assigning vacations in alphabetical order
   B. Find out when the supervisors want to take their vacations, and randomly assign whatever periods are left to the non-supervisory personnel

8.____

C. Assign the most desirable times to employees of longest standing and the least desirable times to the newest employees
D. Have all employees state their own preference, and then work out any conflicts in consultation with the people involved

9. Assume that you have been asked to prepare job descriptions for various positions in your department.
Which of the following are the basic points that should be covered in a *job description*?
   A. General duties and responsibilities of the position, with examples of day-to-day tasks
   B. Comments on the performances of present employees
   C. Estimates of the number of openings that may be available in each category during the coming year
   D. Instructions for carrying out the specific tasks assigned to your department

10. Of the following, the biggest DISADVANTAGE in allowing a free flow of communications in an agency is that such a free flow
    A. decreases creativity
    B. increases the use of the *grapevine*
    C. lengthens the chain of command
    D. reduces the executive's power to direct the flow of information

11. A downward flow of authority in an organization is one example of _____ communication.
    A. horizontal   B. informal   C. circular   D. vertical

12. Of the following, the one that would MOST likely block effective communication is
    A. concentration only on the issues at hand
    B. lack of interest or commitment
    C. use of written reports
    D. use of charts and graphs

13. An ADVANTAGE of the *lecture* as a teaching tool is that it
    A. enables a person to present his ideas to a large number of people
    B. allows the audience to retain a maximum of the information given
    C. holds the attention of the audience for the longest time
    D. enables the audience member to easily recall the main points

14. An ADVANTAGE of the *small-group* discussion as a teaching tool is that
    A. it always focuses attention on one person as the leader
    B. it places collective responsibility on the group as a whole
    C. its members gain experience by summarizing the ideas of others
    D. each member of the group acts as a member of a team

15. The one of the following that is an ADVANTAGE of a *large-group* discussion, when compared to a small-group discussion, is that the large-group discussion
    A. moves along more quickly than a small-group discussion
    B. allows its participants to feel more at ease, and speak out more freely
    C. gives the whole group a chance to exchange ideas on a certain subject at the same occasion
    D. allows its members to feel a greater sense of personal responsibility

15.____

KEY (CORRECT ANSWERS)

1.	D	6.	D	11.	D
2.	C	7.	B	12.	B
3.	D	8.	D	13.	A
4.	D	9.	A	14.	D
5.	C	10.	D	15.	C

EXAMINATION SECTION
TEST 1

DIRECTIONS: Each question or incomplete statement is followed by several suggested answers or completions. Select the one that BEST answers the question or completes the statement. *PRINT THE LETTER OF THE CORRECT ANSWER IN THE SPACE AT THE RIGHT.*

1. Managing conflict effectively by avoiding no-win situations, positively influencing the actions of others and using _____ strategies are what make a great leader. 1._____
    A. persuasive   B. ambiguous   C. prosecution   D. performance

2. In today's business world, collaboration will bring together people from distinct backgrounds. These collaborative groups may not share common norms, morals or _____, but they can offer unique _____. 2._____
    A. vocabulary; perspectives
    B. salaries; vocabulary
    C. modifications; insights
    D. perspectives; salaries

3. E-mail is a great tool for communication; however, which of the following should you be careful of when in electronic communication with a colleague? 3._____
    A. Font size
    B. E-mail length
    C. Font color
    D. Tone of voice

4. A formal relationship can BEST be described as 4._____
    A. regulated by procedures or directives
    B. personal and relaxed
    C. emotionally distant and very uncomfortable
    D. confusing and unproductive

5. John is in a meeting with his supervisor ad coworkers. He is thinking about what he's going to have for dinner that night when his boss asks him a question. John can repeat back what his supervisor said, but he cannot retain what was said during the meeting.
    This is a classic example of failing to 5._____
    A. focus at work
    B. effectively listen
    C. leave personal plans outside the workplace
    D. care about meetings

6. A person's choice of _____ can directly affect communication. 6._____
    A. clothing   B. food   C. hygiene   D. words

7. Why is it important to relax when communicating with team members? 7._____
    A. Relaxing always means having better ideas.
    B. People will automatically like you more if you are relaxed.

C. If you are nervous, you may talk too quickly and make it hard for others to understand your message or directive.
D. No one likes someone who is always working, so it is important to relax and not work too hard.

8. In order to show you are genuinely interested in what others have to say, you should
    A. tell them how nice they are
    B. repeat what they say back to them
    C. nod and find something to compliment them about
    D. ask questions and seek clarification from them

    8.____

9. Jack and James are always arguing with one another. Their supervisor calls each one in separately to talk to them. He asks Jack to think about things from James' point of view and he asks James to do the same for Jack.
    What is the supervisor trying to get each person to do?
    A. Get along   B. Be positive
    C. Communicate effectively   D. Empathize

    9.____

10. When working in groups, disagreements
    A. should be avoided at all costs
    B. are often a healthy way of building understanding and camaraderie
    C. lead coworkers to hate one another and the company they work for
    D. don't happen if the supervisor chooses the right people to work together

    10.____

11. If things go wrong in a group situation, it is important to AVOID
    A. the boss   B. disagreements or arguments
    C. scapegoating   D. being polite and fair to one another

    11.____

12. If you are a listener who likes to hear the rationale behind a message, your listening style would be described as _____ style.
    A. results   B. process   C. reasons   D. eye contact

    12.____

13. Which of the following BEST describes a psychological barrier in communication?
    A. Molly is so stressed about her paying for her mortgage that she can't focus at work right now.
    B. John doesn't understand a lot of the terms the IT specialist used in an e-mail sent out to everyone.
    C. Jerry is a little older and has a hard time hearing everything so sometimes he misses parts of a conversation.
    D. Linda doesn't want to be at the company for longer than a few months, so she doesn't really try too hard to fit in.

    13.____

14. Body language, also known as _____, is really important when building rapport with coworkers and communicating effectively.
    A. verbal language   B. kinesthetic
    C. non-verbal communication   D. facial expressions

    14.____

15. Which of the following might be a good example of someone who has a "closed" posture?
    A. Hands are apart on the arms of the chair.
    B. His/her arms are folded.
    C. They are directly facing you.
    D. They barely speak above a whisper.

16. Which of the following can eye contact be used for?
    A. To give and receive feedback
    B. To let someone know when it is their turn to speak
    C. To communicate how you feel about someone
    D. All of the above

17. Which of the following is NOT a form of non-verbal communication?
    A. Crossing your arms when talking to someone
    B. Using space within the room in a conversation
    C. Clearing your throat before you speak]
    D. Saying "10-4" when asked if you understand

18. Your best friend has just been hired at the company you work for. You notice he has come into work on several occasions after staying out late the night before. His work has not suffered yet, but you fear it will.
    Which of the following actions should you take to help prevent future problems?
    A. Do nothing; he's your friend but it is his life
    B. Try to talk to him and help him see the importance of not creating bad habits.
    C. Talk to your supervisor and tell him your friend isn't suitable for the job
    D. Tell your friend to change his ways or to quit

19. Interacting with coworkers can be positively or negatively affected by _____ when someone's previous biases and assumptions shape their reactions in future situations.
    A. racism
    B. past experience
    C. interpersonal skills
    D. active listening

20. Which of the following scenarios BEST describes a person who is being subjective?
    A. Sally is fair and honest when she listens to coworkers. She does not take sides and wants the best solution to the problem.
    B. Mike doesn't like Steve, because he thinks Steve is only out for himself. Still, Steve offers valuable insights, so Mike tries not to let personal feelings get in the way of working together.
    C. Jamie is dating Veronica's ex and Veronica just found out. Now, Veronica immediately shoots down anything Jamie suggests during a meeting as irrational and superfluous.
    D. None of the above

21. Which important communications tem is MOST closely defined as "the quality of a sound governed by the rate of vibrations producing it; the degree of highness or lowness of a tone"?
    A. Tone
    B. Pitch
    C. Effective communication
    D. Rationalization

21.____

22. _____ is when a person tries to make an imprudent and reckless action seem reasonable.
    A. Projection
    B. Self-deception
    C. Past experience
    D. Rationalization

22.____

23. When holding conversations with coworkers, you should
    A. do most of the talking
    B. let others do most of the talking
    C. try to split time between talking and listening
    D. zone out and wait for the meeting to finish

23.____

24. A new hire just arrived and you are meeting her for the first time. Which of the following actions is MOST appropriate?
    A. Walk up and introduce yourself with a smile and a handshake
    B. Wait for her to come and introduce herself
    C. Approach her and offer a hug to make her feel welcome
    D. Ignore the new hire; she is likely your competition

24.____

25. If you are the type of listener who likes to discuss concepts or issues in detail, you would MOST likely fall under which listening style?
    A. Process
    B. Reasons
    C. Results
    D. None of the above

25.____

KEY (CORRECT ANSWERS)

1. A
2. A
3. D
4. A
5. B

6. D
7. C
8. D
9. D
10. B

11. C
12. C
13. A
14. C
15. B

16. D
17. D
18. B
19. B
20. C

21. B
22. D
23. C
24. A
25. A

TEST 2

DIRECTIONS: Each question or incomplete statement is followed by several suggested answers or completions. Select the one that BEST answers the question or completes the statement. *PRINT THE LETTER OF THE CORRECT ANSWER IN THE SPACE AT THE RIGHT.*

1. Which of the following is an example of the BEST practice when communicating in the workplace?
   A. You are horrible with remembering names so you try to use nicknames to cover up for your poor memory.
   B. You only pay attention to the names of people who you work for or who you deem to be "important."
   C. You try to remember everyone's names and use them whenever possible.
   D. None of the above

   1.____

2. Words of civility such as "please" and "thank you" should be used _____ when conversing with coworkers and business partners.
   A. always   B. sometimes   C. rarely   D. never

   2.____

3. When communicating with others, one should _____ stand as close to them as possible and make body contact in order to get an important point across.
   A. always   B. sometimes   C. rarely   D. never

   3.____

4. The MOST appropriate way to end a conversation is to
   A. seek a mutual resolution, but leave abruptly if it continues
   B. find a way to wrap up the conversation so the other person knows it is time to move on
   C. look impatient so hopefully the person will get the hint
   D. tell the other person the conversation should end

   4.____

5. Another name for interpersonal communication in an office setting is
   A. peer-to-peer communication   B. mass communication
   C. virtual reality   D. e-mailing

   5.____

6. Of the following statements, choose the one you feel is the MOST correct.
   A. Devoid of interpersonal communication, people become sick.
   B. Communication is not completely needed for humans.
   C. People are the only animals that need to have relationships in order to survive.
   D. Important communication is not really relevant until after you become an adult.

   6.____

7. John is giving a presentation on ways to communicate effectively with peers. He is having trouble deciding on what to say in his speech.
   Which of the following statements should he AVOID using?
   A. Always try to understand another person's point of view or perspective
   B. Try to imagine what someone is going to say before they actually say it

   7.____

C. Be aware of how non-verbal cues like eye contact and body language affect how your message is received
D. Both B and C

8. Which of the following would MOST affect our perception of communication with coworkers?
   A. Past experiences
   B. Marital problems
   C. Rumors spread about coworkers
   D. None of the above

9. Many people think of communication as both _____ and _____ messages.
   A. formal; informal
   B. hearing; listening
   C. sending; receiving
   D. finding; decoding

10. Why is context important in communication?
    A. It's important to know which buttons to push in order to get what you want.
    B. Saying something to one person may not have the same effect as saying it to someone else.
    C. Context is only important if you are worried about what others think.
    D. None of the above

11. If your brother is normally bright and talkative during the summer, but you notice he gets quiet and subdued in the winter, the MOST likely communication context he is dealing with would be
    A. relational   B. cultural   C. inner   D. physical

12. _____ is an example of a negative nonverbal action you can take.
    A. Smiling
    B. Using a tone of voice that matches your message
    C. Maintaining eye contact
    D. Slumping your shoulders

13. Cultural context can BEST be described as
    A. what people think of as it relates to the event they are participating in (i.e., wedding versus a funeral)
    B. the connection between a father and his son
    C. rules and patterns of Americans versus the Japanese
    D. thoughts, feelings, and sensations inside a person's head

14. Which of the following BEST describes feedback?
    A. Staring at the speaker while he talks
    B. Nodding and smiling while listening to a speaker
    C. Standing an appropriate distance away so the speaker does not get uncomfortable
    D. Trying to speak while the other person is speaking because you have something more important to say

15. Being able to communicate more effectively can be improved upon by
    A. continually making an effort to be as flexible as possible when talking to others
    B. committing to one style of speaking until you master it
    C. using the same style of correspondence as the person with whom you are speaking
    D. always using the opposite style of communication from the person you are speaking to

16. John walks up to Sally and compliments her on the dress she wore to work today. In his mind, John was just being friendly, but Sally went to her manager and filed a harassment charge against John.
    This miscommunication could MOST easily be classified as an error in what?
    A. Reality B. Perception C. Friendship D. Loyalty

17. If a speaker's tone is flat and monotone, which of the following is the MOST likely reaction that listeners will have?
    They will
    A. enthused by the message
    B. enjoy the message but not be overly excited about it
    C. be polite and interested but will not seem very engaged
    D. be bored and uninterested in the message

18. When Steve speaks to his group about his ideas, he generally has a higher pitch to his voice and gesticulates frequently.
    This lead his team members to believe that Steve
    A. is enthusiastic and has great ideas for the group
    B. has had too much caffeine and needs to relax
    C. is trying to show off for the boss and make them look bad
    D. is extremely smart and great at his job

19. _____ is used when a person wants to add stress to key words in communication. It lets the audience understand the mood or feelings of particular words or phrases.
    A. Anger B. Tone C. Perception D. Inflection

20. If Barry tells Bill that his haircut looks "great" and Bill can tell Barry is being insincere, which of the following tones is Barry MOST likely using?
    A. Affectionate B. Apologetic C. Threatening D. Sarcastic

21. As a supervisor, it is important that everyone clearly comprehends everything you communicate to them.
    In order to ensure this happens, which of the following things should you avoid?
    A. Overusing jargon
    B. Explaining something more than once
    C. Speaking slowly and annunciating everything
    D. Having meetings in the morning

22. If your supervisor is looking down at the ground or has his back to you as he is speaking, it MOST clearly indicates to those who are listening to him that the supervisor
    A. is shy and doesn't like speaking in front of people
    B. is disinterested and doesn't care what he's talking about
    C. is approachable and friendly
    D. dislikes his job and wants to get out as soon as possible

22.____

23. Interpersonal communication helps you
    A. know what others are thinking
    B. turn into an inspiring speaker, especially in public
    C. learn about yourself
    D. communicate with the general public

23.____

24. In general, people who smile more are perceived as
    A. devious
    B. friendly
    C. attractive
    D. easy to manipulate

24.____

25. If your supervisor constantly takes advantage of you and expresses his or her opinion often at the expense of you or other workers, which communication style are they MOST likely using?
    A. Nonassertive   B. Assertive   C. Aggressive   D. Peacemaking

25.____

KEY (CORRECT ANSWERS)

1.	C		11.	D
2.	A		12.	D
3.	D		13.	C
4.	B		14.	B
5.	A		15.	A
6.	A		16.	B
7.	B		17.	D
8.	A		18.	A
9.	C		19.	D
10.	B		20.	D

21. A
22. B
23. D
24. B
25. C

EDUCATING AND INTERACTING WITH THE PUBLIC

These questions test for knowledge of techniques used to interact effectively with individual citizens and/or community groups, to educate or inform them about topics of concern, to publicize or clarify agency programs or policies, to negotiate conflicts or resolve complaints, and to represent one's agency or program in a manner in keeping with good public relations practices. Questions may also cover interacting with others in cooperative efforts of public outreach or service. There will be 15 questions in this subject area on the written test.

TEST TASK:
You will be presented with a variety of situations in which you must apply knowledge of how best to interact with other people.

SAMPLE QUESTION:
A person approaches you expressing anger about a recent action by your department. Which one of the following should be your first response to this person?

   A. Interrupt to say you cannot discuss the situation until he calms down.
   B. Say you are sorry that he has been negatively affected by your department's action.
   C. Listen and express understanding that he has been upset by your department's action.
   D. Give him an explanation of the reasons for your department's action.

The correct answer to this sample question is choice C

C. SOLUTION:

Choice A is not correct. It would be inappropriate to interrupt. In addition, saying that you cannot discuss the situation until the person calms down will likely aggravate him further.

Choice B is not correct. Apologizing for your department's action implies that the action was improper.

Choice C is the correct answer to this question. By listening and expressing understanding that your department's action has upset him, you demonstrate that you have heard and understand his feelings and point of view.

Choice D is not correct. While an explanation of the reasons for the action may be appropriate at a later time, at this moment the person is angry and would not be receptive to such an explanation.

EXAMINATION SECTION
TEST 1

DIRECTIONS: Each question or incomplete statement is followed by several suggested answers or completions. Select the one that BEST answers the question or completes the statement. *PRINT THE LETTER OF THE CORRECT ANSWER IN THE SPACE AT THE RIGHT.*

1. A specialist is meeting with a panel of local community leaders to determine their perceptions about the effectiveness of a recent outreach program. The leaders seem unresponsive to the specialist's questions, looking at the floor or each other without directly answering the specialist's questions.
   One strategy that might work to elicit the desired information would be to
   A. try to discern the hidden meaning of their silence
   B. adopt a mildly confrontational tone and remind them of what's at stake in the community
   C. keep asking open-ended questions and wait patiently for responses
   D. tell them to come back when they're ready to tell you their opinions

   1.____

2. Each of the following statements about maintaining a community's attention is true, EXCEPT:
   A. The more challenging it is to pay attention to a message, the more likely it is that it will be attended to
   B. Listeners will be more motivated to pay attention if a speech is personally meaningful
   C. People will be more likely to attend if a speaker pauses to suggest natural transitions in a speech
   D. Listeners will attend to messages that stand out

   2.____

3. Each of the following is a key strategy to integrative bargaining among community members in conflict, EXCEPT
   A. focusing on positions, rather than interests
   B. separating the people from the problem
   C. aiming for an outcome based on an objectively identified standard
   D. using active listening skills, such as rephrasing and questioning

   3.____

4. Which of the following is NOT one of the major variables to take into account when considering a community needs assessment?
   A. State of program development   B. Resources available
   C. Demographics   D. Community attitudes

   4.____

5. Which of the following groups would probably be formed specifically for, or be involved in, the purpose of addressing a specific unmet community need?
   A. An existing consumer group
   B. A council of community representatives
   C. A committee
   D. An existing community organization

   5.____

6. If a public outreach campaign designed to mobilize a community fails, the MOST likely reason for this failure is that the campaign
    A. was not specific about what it wanted people to do
    B. was overly serious and did not appeal to people's sense of humor
    C. offered no incentive for the audience to make a change
    D. did not use language that appealed to the audience's emotions

7. Nationwide, the rate of involvement of elderly people in community-based programs demonstrates that they are
    A. under-served when compared to other age groups
    B. served at about the same rate as other age groups
    C. over-served when compared to other age groups
    D. hardly served at all

8. In projecting the likelihood of an education program's success, a domestic violence specialist identifies every single event that must occur to complete the project. The specialist then arranges these events in sequential order and allocates time requirements for each. Finally, the total time is calculated and a model showing all their events and timelines is charted.
    The specialist has used
    A. a PERT chart
    B. a simulation
    C. a Markov model
    D. the critical path method

9. When working with members of a predominantly African-American community, specialists from other cultural backgrounds should be aware that African-Americans tend to express thoughts and feelings through descriptions of
    A. physically tangible sensations
    B. problems to be analyzed
    C. corresponding analogies
    D. spiritual issues

10. Local nonprofessionals should be considered useful to a specialist who is looking to undertake a community outreach or educational initiative.
    Which of the following is LEAST likely to be a characteristic or role demonstrated by these community members?
    A. Undertaking support functions at the agency
    B. Serving as a communication channel between the agency and clients
    C. Encouraging greater agency acceptance and credibility within the community
    D. Helping the agency to accomplish meaningful change

11. In working with Native American groups or clients, it is important to recognize that the GREATEST health problem facing their communities today is
    A. domestic violence
    B. depression and suicide
    C. alcoholism
    D. tuberculosis

12. A specialist is facilitating a cooperative conflict resolution session between community members who have different opinions about what kinds of intervention services should be offered by the local adult protective services agency.
    Which of the following is NOT a guideline that should be followed in this process?
    A. Early in the negotiations, ask each party to name the issues on which they will positively not yield.
    B. Try to get the parties to view the issue from other points of view, beside the two or three conflicting ones.
    C. Have each side volunteer what it would be willing to do to resolve the conflict.
    D. At the end of the session, draw up a formal agreement with agreed-upon actions for both parties.

13. A specialist wants to evaluate the effectiveness of a local women's shelter. The shelter has suffered from lax participation, given the number of women who have been abused in the surrounding area. The specialist wants to speak with the women in the community who did not follow up on referrals to the shelter, and begins by visiting some of these women. After gaining the trust of these women, the specialist asks for the names of women they know who might be in need of help with a domestic violence situation.
    The specialist's approach in this case is _____ sampling.
    A. maximum variation   B. snowball
    C. convenience   D. typical case

14. When it comes to perceiving messages, people typically DON'T
    A. tend to simplify causal connections and sometimes even seek a single cause to explain what may be a highly complex effect
    B. tend to perceive messages independently of a categorical framework, especially if the message may be distorted by such an interpretation
    C. have a predisposition toward accepting any pattern that a speaker offers to explain seemingly unconnected facts
    D. tend to interpret things in the way they are viewed by their reference group

15. The elder members of Native American communities, regardless of kinship, are MOST commonly referred to as
    A. the ancients   B. father or mother
    C. grandfather or grandmother D. chiefs

16. Each of the following is typically an objective of community mobilization, EXCEPT:
    A. To convince existing community resources to alter their services or work together to address an unmet need
    B. To gather and distribute information to consumers and agencies about unmet needs

C. To publicize existing community resources and make them more accessible
D. To bring an unmet community need to public attention in order to achieve acceptance of and support for fulfilling the need

17. Research in community outreach shows that women often build friendships through shared positive feelings, whereas men often build friendships through
    A. metacommunication
    B. catharsis
    C. impression management
    D. shared activities

17.____

18. Typically, the FIRST step in a community-needs assessment is to
    A. identify community's strengths
    B. explore the nature of the neighborhood
    C. get to know the area and its residents
    D. talk to people in the community

18.____

19. Most public relations experts agree that _____ exposure(s) to a message is the minimum just to get the message noticed. If the aim of a public outreach campaign is action or a change in behavior, the agency budget must plan for more exposures.
    A. one
    B. two
    C. three
    D. four

19.____

20. In the program development/community liaison model of community work and public outreach, the PRIMARY constituency is considered to be
    A. community representatives and the service agency board or administrators
    B. elected officials, social agencies, and interagency organizations
    C. marginalized or oppressed population groups in a city or region
    D. residents of a neighborhood, parish or rural county

20.____

21. Social or interpersonal problems in many African-American communities have their roots in
    A. personality deficits
    B. unresolved family conflicts
    C. poor communication
    D. external stressors

21.____

22. A public outreach campaign should
    I. focus on short-term, measurable goals, rather than ultimate outcomes
    II. try to alter entrenched attitudes within a short time, with powerfully worded messages
    III. proceed in steps or phases, each of which lays out a mechanism that leads to the desired effect
    IV. ignore causes that led to a problem, and instead focus on solutions

    The CORRECT answer is:
    A. I and II
    B. II and III
    C. III only
    D. I, II, III and IV

22.____

23. Research findings indicate that in listing preferences for helping professional attributes, individuals from culturally diverse groups are MOST likely to consider _____ as more important than _____.
    A. personality similarity; either race/ethnic similarity or attitude similarity
    B. therapist experience; any kind of similarity
    C. race/ethnic similarity; attitude similarity
    D. attitude similarity; race/ethnic similarity

24. Each of the following is considered to be an objective of community organization EXCEPT
    A. effecting changes in the distribution of decision-making power
    B. helping people develop and strengthen the traits of self-direction and cooperation
    C. effecting and maintaining the balance between needs and resources in a community
    D. helping people deal with their problems by developing alternative behaviors

25. A specialist is helping the adult protective services agency to design a public outreach campaign. The topic to be addressed is complex, public understanding is low, and most professionals at the agency feel that having more complete information might change the opinions of community members. Which method of pre-campaign research is probably MOST appropriate?
    A. Deliberative polling
    B. Attitude scales
    C. Surveys or questionnaires
    D. Focus groups

KEY (CORRECT ANSWERS)

1.	C		11.	C
2.	A		12.	A
3.	A		13.	B
4.	C		14.	B
5.	C		15.	C
6.	A		16.	B
7.	A		17.	D
8.	D		18.	B
9.	C		19.	C
10.	A		20.	A

21. D
22. C
23. D
24. D
25. A

TEST 2

DIRECTIONS: Each question or incomplete statement is followed by several suggested answers or completions. Select the one that BEST answers the question or completes the statement. *PRINT THE LETTER OF THE CORRECT ANSWER IN THE SPACE AT THE RIGHT.*

1. A specialist has been called in to resolve a dispute between two community leaders who have been arguing about the level of service needed within the community. The discussion has been going on for several hours when the specialist arrives, and both people seem to be upset.
After calming the two down and getting each of them to agree on a statement of the problem, the specialist should ask each person to
    A. summarize his or her argument in three main points
    B. explain why he or she became so upset
    C. clearly state, in objective terms, the position of the other in a form that meets with the other's approval
    D. identify the best alternative outcome, other than their presumed ideal

    1.____

2. In evaluating the impact of a public outreach campaign, the _____ model can be used early in the campaign to address first impressions.
    A. exposure or advertising
    B. expert interview
    C. impact monitoring or process
    D. experimental or quasi-experimental

    2.____

3. When trying to motivate an older population to take action on a community problem, it is helpful to remember that older people
    A. are more self-reliant in their decision-making than other members of the same family
    B. often need more time to decide than younger people
    C. are more likely than younger people to view community problems self-referentially
    D. tend to take a pragmatic, rather than philosophical, view of life

    3.____

4. The method of group or community decision-making that is normally MOST time-consuming is
    A. majority opinion   B. consensus
    C. expert opinion   D. authority rule

    4.____

5. A local adult protective services agency has identified one of the goals of its recent public outreach campaign to be the mobilization of activists.
The campaign should probably
    A. target neutral audiences
    B. home in on supporters
    C. stick to purely factual information
    D. try to persuade community fence-sitters

    5.____

6. Research of Native American youths' perceptions of family concerns for their well-being has generally found that these youths
   A. have a high degree of uncertainty about their families' feelings toward them
   B. believe their families don't care about them
   C. believe that their mothers care a great deal about them, but their fathers don't
   D. believe their families care a great deal about them

7. A domestic violence specialist is developing a new outreach program for the local community. The specialist has defined the target problem, set program goals, and planned the actions that will take place as a result of the program. Most likely, the next step will be to
   A. evaluate the resources available to achieve program goals
   B. define and sequence the steps that will be taken to achieve program goals
   C. determine how the program will be evaluated
   D. decide how the program will operate

8. Elder: *I'm so glad to have someone to talk to, someone who really understands my problem.*
   Specialist: *It is nice to be able to talk to someone who will listen.*
   Elder: *That's for sure.*
   In the above exchange, what listening skill is evident in the underlined statement?
   A. Verbatim response
   B. Paraphrasing
   C. Advising
   D. Evaluation

9. Which of the following activities is involved in the specialist's task of mobilizing?
   A. Meeting individuals in the community with problems and assisting them in finding help
   B. Identifying unmet community needs
   C. Speaking out against an unjust policy or procedure
   D. Developing new services or linking presently available services to meet community needs

10. The preliminary research associated with a public outreach campaign should FIRST be aimed at determining
    A. the budget
    B. the message's ultimate audience
    C. what media to use
    D. the short-term behavioral goals of the campaign

11. A specialist in a low-income community wants to plan programs that will deal with the influence of unemployment on domestic disturbances. The specialist needs to know not only how many unemployed people are in the community now, but also how many people will be unemployed at any particular tie in the future, and how those numbers will vary given certain conditions.

Probably the BEST way to trace employment rates over time and within differing conditions is through the use of
- A. the critical path
- B. linear programming
- C. difference equations
- D. the Markov model

12. Generally, public outreach programs—whatever their stated goal—should
    I. create a sense of urgency about a problem
    II. decline to identify opponents of the issue or idea
    III. propose concrete, easily understandable solutions
    IV. urge a specific action

    The CORRECT answer is:
    A. I only   B. I, III and IV   C. II and III   D. I, II, III and IV

13. Which of the following methods of community needs assessment relies to the GREATEST degree on existing public records?
    - A. Social indicators
    - B. Field study
    - C. Rates under treatment
    - D. Key informant

14. During an interview with a Native American client, a specialist is careful to maintain close and nearly constant eye contact.
    The client is MOST likely to interpret this as a(n)
    - A. show of high concern
    - B. sign of disrespect
    - C. uncomfortable assumption of intimacy
    - D. attempt to intimidate

15. The BEST strategy for addressing an audience that is known to be captive, or even hostile, is to
    - A. refer to experiences in common
    - B. flatter the audience
    - C. joke about things in or near the audience
    - D. plead for fairness

16. Integrative conflict resolution is characterized by
    - A. an overriding concern to maximize joint outcomes
    - B. one side's interests opposing the other's
    - C. a fixed and limited amount of resources to be divided, so that the more one group gets, the less another gets
    - D. manipulation and withholding information as negotiation strategies

17. A specialist wants to learn how to interact with the members of a largely Latino community in a more culturally sensitive way.
    Which of the following is NOT a guideline for interacting with members of a Latino community?
    - A. Efforts to foster independence and self-reliance may be interpreted by many Latinos as a lack of concern for others.
    - B. Efforts to deal one-on-one with an adolescent client may serve to alienate the parents, especially the mother.

C. A nonverbal gesture, such as lowering the eyes, is interpreted by many Latinos as a sign of respect and deference to authority.
D. In much of Latino culture, the focus of control for problems tends to be much more external than internal.

18. Each of the following is a supporting assumption of community organization, EXCEPT:
    A. Democracy requires cooperative participation.
    B. In order for communities to change, it is necessary for each individual in the community to be willing to change.
    C. Communities often need help with organization and planning.
    D. Holistic approaches work better than fragmented or ad-hoc programs.

19. Helping professionals often have difficulty to bring community resources together to fulfill unmet community needs.
    Which of the following is NOT usually a reason for this?
    A. Some community groups resist assistance when it is offered.
    B. Few community groups make their needs known.
    C. Community resources frequently change the type of services they offer.
    D. Often, community resources prefer to work alone.

20. When dealing with groups or populations of elderly clients, specialists should be mindful that about _____ of the nation's elderly suffer from mental health problems.
    A. a tenth   B. a quarter   C. a third   D. half

21. In an African-American community, a specialist from another culture should recognize that church participation, for most African-Americans, is viewed as a
    A. method for maintaining control and communicating competency
    B. way of depersonalizing problems or troubles
    C. way to divert attention away from problems
    D. means of cathartic emotional release

22. Adult protective service programs supported by state statutes protect elderly people from abuse and neglect under the doctrine of
    A. parens patriae   B. habeas corpus
    C. in loco parentis   D. volenti non fit injuria

23. In terms of public outreach, which of the following statements about an audience is NOT generally true?
    A. The more heterogeneous the audience, the more necessary it will be to use specific examples and appeals to certain types of people.
    B. The smaller the audience, the more likely that its members will share assumptions and values.
    C. When the speaker does not know the status of an audience, it is best to assume that they are captive rather than voluntary.
    D. The larger an audience, the more formal a presentation is likely to be.

24. A specialist often spends time in the places frequented by community residents. She listens carefully to what residents seem most concerned about, and engages many in conversations, asking them how they see the problems in the community. During these conversations, she makes mental notes about whether the statements of the problems are the same things that are mentioned in their conversations. From these conversations, the worker determines what she thinks the unmet needs of the community are.
Which of the key issues in identifying unmet needs has the worker neglected to address?
    A. The different points of view regarding the issues, and whether there is any common ground
    B. Whether the stated problems and conversations with community residents reflect the same concerns
    C. How community residents define the issues
    D. What the residents talk about with one another in a community

25. Which of the following political styles should be used to promote an issue that could become controversial if it is perceived to involve major reforms?
    A. High-conflict, polarized
    B. High-conflict, consensual
    C. Moderate conflict, compromise-oriented
    D. Low-conflict, technical

KEY (CORRECT ANSWERS)

1.	C		11.	D
2.	A		12.	B
3.	B		13.	A
4.	B		14.	B
5.	B		15.	A
6.	D		16.	A
7.	A		17.	D
8.	B		18.	B
9.	D		19.	C
10.	B		20.	B

21. D
22. A
23. A
24. A
25. D

INTERVIEWING
EXAMINATION SECTION
TEST 1

DIRECTIONS: Each question or incomplete statement is followed by several suggested answers or completions. Select the one that BEST answers the question or completes the statement. *PRINT THE LETTER OF THE CORRECT ANSWER IN THE SPACE AT THE RIGHT.*

1. Of the methods given below for obtaining desired information from applicants, the one considered the BEST interviewing method is to
   A. work from an outline, asking the questions in the order in which they appear and requiring the applicant to give specific answers
   B. let the applicant tell what he has to say in his own way first, the interviewer then taking responsibility for asking questions on points not covered
   C. tell the applicant all the facts that it is necessary to have, then letting him give the information in any way he chooses
   D. verify all such facts as birth date, income, and past employment before seeing the applicant, then asking the applicant to fill in the remaining gaps when he is interviewed

2. Suppose an applicant objects to answering a question regarding his recent employment and asks, "What business is it of yours, young man?"
   In conducting the interview, the MOST constructive course of action for you to take under the circumstances would be to
   A. tell the applicant you have no intention of prying into his personal affairs and go on to the next question
   B. refer the applicant to your supervisor
   C. rephrase the question so that only a "Yes" or "No" answer is required
   D. explain why the question is being asked

3. An interview is BEST conducted in private PRIMARILY because
   A. the person interviewed will tend to be less self-conscious
   B. the interviewer will be able to maintain his continuity of thought better
   C. it will insure that the interview is "off the record"
   D. people tend to "show off" before an audience

4. An interviewer will be better able to understand the person interviewed and his problems if he recognizes that much of the person's behavior is due to motives
   A. which are deliberate   B. of which he is unaware
   C. which are inexplicable   D. which are kept under control

5. When an applicant is repeatedly told that "everything will be all right," the effect that can USUALLY be expected is that he will
   A. develop overt negativistic reactions toward the agency
   B. become too closely identified with the interviewer
   C. doubt the interviewer's ability to understand and help with his problems
   D. have greater confidence in the interviewer

6. While interviewing a client, it is PREFERABLE that the interviewer
   A. take no notes in order to avoid disturbing the client
   B. focus primary attention on the client while the client is talking
   C. take no notes in order to impress upon the client the interviewer's ability to remember all the pertinent facts of his case
   D. record all the details in order to show the client that what he says is important

7. During an interview, a curious applicant asks several questions about the interviewer's private life.
   As the interviewer, you should
   A. refuse to answer such questions
   B. answer his questions fully
   C. explain that your primary concern is with his problems and that discussion of your personal affairs will not be helpful in meeting his needs
   D. explain that it is the responsibility of the interviewer to ask questions and not to answer them

8. An interviewer can BEST establish a good relationship with the person being interviewed by
   A. assuming casual interest in the statements made by the person being interviewed
   B. asking questions which enable the person to show pride in his knowledge
   C. taking the point of view of the person interviewed
   D. showing a genuine interest in the person

9. An interviewer's attention must be directed toward himself as well as toward the person interviewed.
   This statement means that the interviewer should
   A. keep in mind the extent to which his own prejudices may influence his judgment
   B. rationalize the statements made by the person interviewed
   C. gain the respect and confidence of the person interviewed
   D. avoid being too impersonal

10. More complete expression will be obtained from a person being interviewed if the interviewer can create the impression that
    A. the data secured will become part of a permanent record
    B. official information must be accurate in every detail
    C. it is the duty of the person interviewed to give accurate data
    D. the person interviewed is participating in a discussion of his own problems

11. The practice of asking leading questions should be avoided in an interview because the
    A. interviewer risks revealing his attitudes to the person being interviewed
    B. interviewer may be led to ignore the objective attitudes of the person interviewed
    C. answers may be unwarrantedly influenced
    D. person interviewed will resent the attempt to lead him and will be less cooperative

12. A good technique for the interviewer to use in an effort to secure reliable data and to reduce the possibility of misunderstanding is to
    A. use casual undirected conversation, enabling the person being interviewed to talk about himself, and thus secure the desired information
    B. adopt the procedure of using direct questions regularly
    C. extract the desired information from the person being interviewed by putting him on the defensive
    D. explain to the person being interviewed the information desired and the reason for needing it

13. In interviewing an applicant, your attitude toward his veracity should be that the information he has furnished you is
    A. *untruthful* until you have had an opportunity to check the information
    B. *truthful* only insofar as verifiable facts are concerned
    C. *untruthful* because clients tend to interpret everything in their own favor
    D. *truthful* until you have information to the contrary

14. When an agency assigns its most experienced interviewers to conduct initial interviews with applicants, the MOST important reason for its action is that
    A. experienced workers are always older and, therefore, command the respect of applicants
    B. the applicant may be given a complete understanding of the procedures to be followed and the time involved in obtaining assistance
    C. applicants with fraudulent intentions will be detected, and prevented from obtaining further services from the agency
    D. the applicant may be given an understanding of the purpose of the assistance program and of the bases for granting assistance, in addition to the routine information

15. In conducting the first interview with an applicant, you should
    A. ask questions requiring "Yes" or "No" answers in order to simplify the interview
    B. rephrase several of the key questions as a check on his previous statements
    C. let him tell his own story while keeping him to the relevant facts
    D. avoid showing any sympathy for the applicant while he is revealing his personal needs and problems

16. When an interview opens an interview by asking the client direct questions about his work, it is very likely that the client will feel
    A. that the interview is interested in him
    B. at ease if his work has been good
    C. free to discuss his attitudes toward his work
    D. that good reports are of great importance to the interviewer in his thinking

17. When an interviewer does NOT understand the meaning of a response that a client has made, the interviewer should
    A. proceed to another topic
    B. state that he does not understand and ask for clarification
    C. act as if he understands so that the client's confidence in him should not be shaken
    D. ask the client to rephrase his response

18. When an interviewer makes a response which brings on a high degree of resistance in the client, he should
    A. apologize and rephrase his remark in a less evocative manner
    B. accept the resistance on the part of the client
    C. ignore the client's resistance
    D. recognize that little more will be accomplished in the interview and suggest another appointment

19. Most definitions of interviewing would NOT include the following as a necessary aspect:
    A. The interviewer and client meet face-to-face and talk things out
    B. The client is experiencing considerable emotional disturbance
    C. A valuable learning opportunity is provided for the client
    D. The interviewer brings a special competence to the relationship

20. A powerful dynamic in the interviewing process and often the very *antonym* of its counterpart in the instructional process is
    A. encouraging accuracy
    B. emphasizing structure
    C. pointing up sequential and orderly thinking
    D. processing ambiguity and equivocation

21. Interviewing techniques are frequently useful in working with clients.
    A basic fundamental is an atmosphere which may BEST be described as
    A. non-threatening
    B. motivating for creativity
    C. highly charged to stimulate excitement
    D. fairly-well structured

22. In interviewing the disadvantaged client, the subtle technique of steering away from high-level educational and vocational plans must be *replaced* by
    A. a wait-and-see explanation to the client
    B. the use of prediction tables to determine possibilities and probabilities of overcoming this condition

C. avoidance in discussing controversial issues of deprivation
D. encouragement and concrete consideration for planning his future

23. The process of collecting, analyzing, synthesizing, and interpreting information about the client should be
    A. completed prior to interviewing
    B. completed early in the interviewing process
    C. limited to a type of interviewing which is primarily diagnostic in purpose
    D. continuously pursued throughout interviewing

24. Catharsis, the "emotional unloading" of the client's feelings, has a value in the early stages of interviewing because it accomplishes all BUT which one of the following goals?
    It
    A. relieves strong physiological tensions in the client
    B. increases the client's anxiety and aggrandizes his motivation to continue counseling
    C. provides a strong substitute for "acting out" the client's feelings
    D. releases emotional energy which the client has been using to bulwark his defenses

25. In the interviewing process, the interviewer should *usually* give information
    A. whenever it is needed
    B. at the end of the process
    C. in the introductory interview
    D. just before the client would ordinarily request it

KEY (CORRECT ANSWERS)

1.	B	11.	C
2.	D	12.	D
3.	A	13.	D
4.	B	14.	D
5.	C	15.	C
6.	B	16.	D
7.	C	17.	B
8.	D	18.	B
9.	A	19.	B
10.	D	20.	D

21. A
22. D
23. D
24. B
25. A

TEST 2

DIRECTIONS: Each question or incomplete statement is followed by several suggested answers or completions. Select the one that BEST answers the question or completes the statement. *PRINT THE LETTER OF THE CORRECT ANSWER IN THE SPACE AT THE RIGHT.*

1. Of the following problems that might affect the conduct and outcome of an interview, the MOST troublesome and usually the MOST difficult for the interviewer to control is the
    A. tendency of the interviewee to anticipate the needs and preferences of the interviewer
    B. impulse to cut the interviewee off when he seems to have reached the end of an idea
    C. tendency of interviewee attitude to bias the results
    D. tendency of the interviewer to do most of the talking

1.____

2. The supervisor MOST likely to be a good interviewer is one who
    A. is adept at manipulating people and circumstances toward his objective
    B. is able to put himself in the position of the interviewee
    C. gets the more difficult questions out of the way at the beginning of the interview
    D. develops one style and technique that can be used in any type of interview

2.____

3. A good interviewer guards against the tendency to form an overall opinion about an interviewee on the basis of a single aspect of the interviewee's makeup.
   This statement refers to a well-known source of error in interviewing known as the
    A. assumption error   B. expectancy error
    C. extension effect   D. halo effect

3.____

4. In conducting an "exit interview" with an employee who is leaving voluntarily, the interview's MAIN objective should be to
    A. see that the employee leaves with a good opinion of the organization
    B. learn the true reasons for the employee's resignation
    C. find out if the employee would consider a transfer
    D. try to get the employee to remain on the job

4.____

5. During an interview, an interviewee unexpectedly discloses a relevant but embarrassing personal fact.
   It would be BEST for the interviewer to
    A. listen calmly, avoiding any gesture or facial expression that would suggest approval or disapproval of what is related
    B. change the subject, since further discussion in this area may reveal other embarrassing, but irrelevant, personal facts

5.____

C. apologize to the interviewee for having led him to reveal such a fact and promise not to do so again
D. bring the interview to a close as quickly as possible in order to avoid a discussion which may be distressing to the interviewee

6. Suppose that, while you are interviewing an applicant for a position in your office, you notice a contradiction in facts in two of his responses.
For you to call the contradictions to his attention would be
   A. *inadvisable*, because it reduces the interviewee's level of participation
   B. *advisable*, because getting the facts is essential to a successful interview
   C. *inadvisable*, because the interviewer should use more subtle techniques to resolve any discrepancies
   D. *advisable*, because the interviewee should be impressed with the necessity for giving consistent answers

6.____

7. An interviewer should be aware that an undesirable result of including "leading questions" in an interview is to
   A. cause the interviewee to give a "yes" or "no" answers with qualification or explanation
   B. encourage the interviewee to discuss irrelevant topics
   C. encourage the interviewee to give more meaningful information
   D. reduce the validity of the information obtained from the interviewee

7.____

8. The kind of interview which is particularly helpful in getting an employee to tell about his complaints and grievances is one in which
   A. a pattern has been worked out involving a sequence of exact questions to be asked
   B. the interviewee is expected to support his statements with specific evidence
   C. the interviewee is not made to answer specific questions but is encouraged to talk freely
   D. the interviewer has specific items on which he wishes to get or give information

8.____

9. Suppose you are scheduled to interview an employee under your supervision concerning a health problem. You know that some of the questions you will be asking him will seem embarrassing to him, and that he may resist answering these questions.
In general, to hold these questions for the last part of the interview would be
   A. *desirable*; the intervening time period gives the interviewer an opportunity to plan how to ask these sensitive questions.
   B. *undesirable*; the employee will probably feel that he has been tricked when he suddenly must answer embarrassing questions
   C. *desirable*; the employee will probably have increased confidence in the interviewer and be more willing to answer these questions
   D. *undesirable*; questions that are important should not be deferred until the end of the interview

9.____

10. In conducting an interview, the BEST types of questions with which to begin the interview are those which the person interviewed is
    A. willing and able to answer
    B. willing but unable to answer
    C. able but unwilling to answer
    D. unable and unwilling to answer

11. In order to determine accurately a child's age, it is BEST for an interviewer to rely on
    A. the child's grade in school
    B. what the mother says
    C. birth records
    D. a library card

12. In his first interview with a new employee, it would be LEAST appropriate for a unit supervisor to
    A. find out the employee's preference for the several types of jobs to which he is able to assign him
    B. determine whether the employee will make good promotion material
    C. inform the employee of what his basic job responsibilities will be
    D. inquire about the employee's education and previous employment

13. If an interviewer takes care to phrase his questions carefully and precisely, the result will MOST probably be that
    A. he will be able to determine whether the person interviewed is being truthful
    B. the free flow of the interview will be lost
    C. he will get the information he wants
    D. he will ask stereotyped questions and narrow the scope of the interview

14. When, during an interview, is the person interviewed LEAST likely to be cautious about what he tells the interviewer?
    A. Shortly after the beginning when the questions normally suggest pleasant associations to the person interviewed
    B. As long as the interviewer keeps his questions to the point
    C. At the point where the person interviewed gains a clear insight into the area being discussed
    D. When the interview appears formally ended and goodbyes are being said

15. In an interview held for the purpose of getting information from the person interviewed, it is sometimes desirable for the interviewer to repeat the answer he has received to a question.
    For the interviewer to rephrase such an answer in his own words is good practice MAINLY because it
    A. gives the interviewer time to make up his next question
    B. gives the person interviewed a chance to correct any possible misunderstanding
    C. gives the person interviewed the feeling that the interviewer considers his answer important
    D. prevents the person interviewed from changing his answer

16. There are several methods of formulating questions during an interview. The particular method used should be adapted to the interview problems presented by the person being questioned.
    Of the following methods of formulating questions during an interview, the ACCEPTABLE one is for the interviewer to ask questions which
    A. incorporate several items in order to allow a cooperative interviewee freedom to organize his statements
    B. are ambiguous in order to foil a distrustful interviewee
    C. suggest the correct answer in order to assist an interviewee who appears confused
    D. would help an otherwise unresponsive interviewee to become more responsive

16.____

17. For an interviewer to permit the person being interviewed to read the data the interviewer writes as he records the person's responses on a routine departmental form is
    A. *desirable*, because it serves to assure the person interviewed that his responses are being recorded accurately
    B. *undesirable*, because it prevents the interviewer from clarifying uncertain points by asking additional questions
    C. *desirable*, because it makes the time that the person interviewed must wait while the answer is written seem shorter
    D. *undesirable*, because it destroys the confidentiality of the interview

17.____

18. Of the following methods of conducting an interview, the BEST is to
    A. ask questions with "yes" or "no" answers
    B. listen carefully and ask only questions that are pertinent
    C. fire questions at the interviewee so that he must answer sincerely and briefly
    D. read standardized questions to the person being interviewed

18.____

KEY (CORRECT ANSWERS)

1.	A	11.	C
2.	B	12.	B
3.	D	13.	C
4.	B	14.	D
5.	A	15.	B
6.	B	16.	D
7.	D	17.	A
8.	C	18.	B
9.	C		
10.	A		

PREPARING WRITTEN MATERIAL

PARAGRAPH REARRANGEMENT
COMMENTARY

The sentences that follow are in scrambled order. You are to rearrange them in proper order and indicate the letter choice containing the correct answer at the space at the right.

Each group of sentences in this section is actually a paragraph presented in scrambled order. Each sentence in the group has a place in that paragraph; no sentence is to be left out. You are to read each group of sentences and decide upon the best order in which to put the sentences so as to form a well-organized paragraph.

The questions in this section measure the ability to solve a problem when all the facts relevant to its solution are not given.

More specifically, certain positions of responsibility and authority require the employee to discover connection between events sometimes, apparently, unrelated. In order to do this, the employee will find it necessary to correctly infer that unspecified events have probably occurred or are likely to occur. This ability becomes especially important when action must be taken on incomplete information.

Accordingly, these questions require competitors to choose among several suggested alternatives, each of which presents a different sequential arrangement of the events. Competitors must choose the MOST logical of the suggested sequences.

In order to do so, they may be required to draw on general knowledge to infer missing concepts or events that are essential to sequencing the given events. Competitors should be careful to infer only what is essential to the sequence. The plausibility of the wrong alternatives will always require the inclusion of unlikely events or of additional chains of events which are NOT essential to sequencing the given events.

It's very important to remember that you are looking for the best of the four possible choices, and that the best choice of all may not even be one of the answers you're given to choose from.

There is no one right way to solve these problems. Many people have found it helpful to first write out the order of the sentences, as they would have arranged them, on their scrap paper before looking at the possible answers. If their optimum answer is there, this can save them some time. If it isn't, this method can still give insight into solving the problem. Others find it most helpful to just go through each of the possible choices, contrasting each as they go along. You should use whatever method feels comfortable and works for you.

While most of these types of questions are not that difficult, we've added a higher percentage of the difficult type, just to give you more practice. Usually there are only one or two questions on this section that contain such subtle distinctions that you're unable to answer confidently. And you then may find yourself stuck deciding between two possible choices, neither of which you're sure about.

EXAMINATION SECTION

TEST 1

DIRECTIONS: The following groups of sentences need to be arranged in an order that makes sense. Select the letter preceding the sequence that represents the BEST sentence order. *PRINT THE LETTER OF THE CORRECT ANSWER IN THE SPACE AT THE RIGHT.*

1. I. The keyboard was purposely designed to be a little awkward to slow typists down.
    II. The arrangement of letters on the keyboard of a typewriter was not designed for the convenience of the typist.
    III. Fortunately, no one is suggesting that a new keyboard be designed right away.
    IV. If one were, we would have to learn to type all over again.
    V. The reason was that the early machines were slower than the typists and would jam easily.
    The CORRECT answer is:
    A. I, III, IV, II, V
    B. II, V, I, IV, III
    C. V, I, II, III, IV
    D. II, I, V, III, IV

    1.____

2. I. The majority of the new service jobs are part-time or low-paying.
    II. According to the U.S. Bureau of Labor Statistics, jobs in the service sector constitute 72% of all jobs in this country.
    III. If more and more workers receive less and less money, who will buy the goods and services needed to keep the economy going?
    IV. The service sector is by far the fastest growing part of the United States economy.
    V. Some economists look upon this trend with great concern.
    The CORRECT answer is:
    A. II, IV, I, V, III
    B. II, III, IV, I, V
    C. V, IV, II, III, I
    D. III, I, II, IV, V

    2.____

3. I. They can also affect one's endurance.
    II. This can stabilize blood sugar levels, and ensure that the brain is receiving a steady, constant, supply of glucose, so that one is *hitting on all cylinders* while taking the test.
    III. By food, we mean real food, not junk food or unhealthy snacks.
    IV. For this reason, it is important not to skip a meal, and to bring food with you to the exam.
    V. One's blood sugar levels can affect how clearly one is able to think and concentrate during an exam.
    The CORRECT answer is:
    A. V, IV, II, III, I
    B. V, II, I, IV, III
    C. V, I, IV, III, II
    D. V, IV, I, III, II

    3.____

115

4. I. Those who are the embodiment of desire are absorbed in material quests, and those who are the embodiment of feeling are warriors who value power more than possession.
    II. These qualities are in everyone, but in different degrees.
    III. But those who value understanding yearn not for goods or victory, but for knowledge.
    IV. According to Plato, human behavior flows from three main sources: desire, emotion, and knowledge.
    V. In the perfect state, the industrial forces would produce but not rule, the military would protect but not rule, and the forces of knowledge, the philosopher kings, would reign.
    The CORRECT answer is:
    A. IV, V, I, II, III   B. V, I, II, III, IV
    C. IV, III, II, I, V   D. IV, II, I, III, V

5. I. Of the more than 26,000 tons of garbage produced daily in New York City, 12,000 tons arrive daily at Fresh Kills.
    II. In a month, enough garbage accumulates there to fill the Empire State Building.
    III. In 1937, the Supreme Court halted the practice of dumping the trash of New York City into the sea.
    IV. Although the garbage is compacted, in a few years the mounds of garbage at Fresh Kills will be the highest points south of Maine's Mount Desert Island on the Eastern Seaboard.
    V. Instead, tugboats now pull barges of much of the trash to Staten Island and the largest landfill in the world, Fresh Kills.
    The CORRECT answer is:
    A. III, V, IV, I, II   B. III, V, II, IV, I
    C. III, V, I, II, IV   D. III, II, V, IV, I

6. I. Communists rank equality very high, but freedom very low.
    II. Unlike communists, conservatives place a high value on freedom and a very low value on equality.
    III. A recent study demonstrated that one way to classify people's political beliefs is to look at the importance placed on two words: freedom and equality.
    IV. Thus, by demonstrating how members of these groups feel about the two words, the study has proved to be useful for political analysts in several European countries.
    V. According to the study, socialists and liberals rank both freedom and equality very high, while fascists rate both very low.
    The CORRECT answer is:
    A. III, V, I, II, IV   B. V, IV, III, I, II
    C. III, V, IV, II, I   D. III, I, II, IV, V

7.
I. "Can there be anything more amazing than this?"
II. If the riddle is successfully answered, his dead brothers will be brought back to life.
III. "Even though man sees those around him dying every day," says Dharmaraj, "he still believes and acts as if he were immortal."
IV. "What is the cause of ceaseless wonder?" asks the Lord of the Lake.
V. In the ancient epic, <u>The Mahabharata</u>, a riddle is asked of one of the Pandava brothers.
The CORRECT answer is:
A. V, II, I, IV, III
B. V, IV, III, I, II
C. V, II, IV, III, I
D. V, II, IV, I, III

8.
I. On the contrary, the two main theories—the cooperative (neoclassical) theory and the radical (labor theory)—clearly rest on very different assumptions, which have very different ethical overtones.
II. The distribution of income is the primary factor in determining the relative levels of material well-being that different groups or individuals attain.
III. Of all issues in economics, the distribution of income is one of the most controversial.
IV. The neoclassical theory tends to support the existing income distribution (or minor changes), while the labor theory ends to support substantial changes in the way income is distributed.
V. The intensity of the controversy reflects the fact that different economic theories are not purely neutral, *detached* theories with no ethical or moral implications.
The CORRECT answer is:
A. II, I, V, IV, III
B. III, II, V, I, IV
C. III, V, II, I, IV
D. III, V, IV, I, II

9.
I. The pool acts as a broker and ensures that the cheapest power gets used first.
II. Every six seconds, the pool's computer monitors all of the generating stations in the state and decides which to ask for more power and which to cut back.
III. The buying and selling of electrical power is handled by the New York Power Pool in Guilderland, New York.
IV. This is to the advantage of both the buying and selling utilities.
V. The pool began operation in 1970, and consists of the state's eight electric utilities.
The CORRECT answer is:
A. V, I, II, III, IV
B. IV, II, I, III, V
C. III, V, I, IV, II
D. V, III, IV, II, I

10.
   I. Modern English is much simpler grammatically than Old English.
   II. Finnish grammar is very complicated; there are some fifteen cases, for example.
   III. Chinese, a very old language, may seem to be the exception, but it is the great number of characters/words that must be mastered that makes it so difficult to learn, not its grammar.
   IV. The newest literary language—that is, written as well as spoken—is Finish, whose literary roots go back only to about the middle of the nineteenth century.
   V. Contrary to popular belief, the longer a language is been in use the simpler its grammar—not the reverse.

   The CORRECT answer is:
   A. IV, I, II, III, V
   B. V, I, IV, II, III
   C. I, II, IV, III, V
   D. IV, II, III, I, V

10.____

KEY (CORRECT ANSWERS)

1. D
2. A
3. C
4. D
5. C
6. A
7. C
8. B
9. C
10. B

TEST 2

DIRECTIONS: This type of question tests your ability to recognize accurate paraphrasing, well-constructed paragraphs, and appropriate style and tone. It is important that the answer you select contains only the facts or concepts given in the original sentences. It is also important that you be aware of incomplete sentences, inappropriate transitions, unsupported opinions, incorrect usage, and illogical sentence order. Paragraphs that do not include all the necessary facts and concepts, that distort them, or that add new ones are not considered correct.

The format for this section may vary. Sometimes, long paragraphs are given, and emphasis is placed on style and organization. Our first five questions are of this type. Other times, the paragraphs are shorter, and there is less emphasis on style and more emphasis on accurate representation of information. Our second group of five questions are of this nature.

For each of Questions 1 through 10, select the paragraph that BEST expresses the ideas contained in the sentences above it. *PRINT THE LETTER OF THE CORRECT ANSWER IN THE SPACE AT THE RIGHT.*

1. I. Listening skills are very important for managers.
   II. Listening skills are not usually emphasized.
   III. Whenever managers are depicted in books, manuals or the media, they are always talking, never listening.
   IV. We'd like you to read the enclosed handout on listening skills and to try to consciously apply them this week.
   V. We guarantee they will improve the quality of your interactions.

   1.____

   A. Unfortunately, listening skills are not usually emphasized for managers. Managers are always depicted as talking, never listening. We'd like you to read the enclosed handout on listening skills. Please try to apply these principles this week. If you do, we guarantee they will improve the quality of your interactions.
   B. The enclosed handout on listening skills will be important improving the quality of your interactions. We guarantee it. All you have to do is take sometime this week to read and to consciously try to apply the principles. Listening skills are very important for manages, but they are not usually emphasized. Whenever managers are depicted in books, manuals or the media, they are always talking, never listening.
   C. Listening well is one of the most important skills a manager can have, yet it's not usually given much attention. Think about any representation of managers in books, manuals, or in the media that you may have seen. They're always talking, never listening. We'd like you to read the enclosed handout on listening skills and consciously try to apply them the rest of the week. We guarantee you will see a difference in the quality of your interactions.

119

D. Effective listening, one very important tool in the effective manager's arsenal, is usually not emphasized enough. The usual depiction of managers in books, manuals or the media is one in which they are always talking, never listening. We'd like you to read the enclosed handout and consciously try to apply the information contained therein throughout the rest of the week. We feel sure that you will see a marked difference in the quality of your interactions.

2.
I. Chekhov wrote three dramatic masterpieces which share certain themes and formats: Uncle Vanya, The Cherry Orchard, and The Three Sisters.
II. They are primarily concerned with the passage of time and how this erodes human aspirations.
III. The plays are haunted by the ghosts of the wasted life.
IV. The characters are concerned with life's lesser problems; however, such as the inability to make decisions, loyalty to the wrong cause, and the inability to be clear.
V. This results in sweet, almost aching, type of a sadness referred to as Chekhovian.

2.____

   A. Chekhov wrote three dramatic masterpieces: Uncle Vanya, The Cherry Orchard, and The Three Sisters. These masterpieces share certain themes and formats: the passage of time, how time erodes human aspirations, and the ghosts of wasted life. Each masterpiece is characterized by a sweet, almost aching, type of sadness that has become known as Chekhovian. The sweetness of this sadness hinges on the fact that it is not the great tragedies of life which are destroying these characters, but their minor flaws: indecisiveness, misplaced loyalty, unclarity.
   B. The Cherry Orchard, Uncle Vanya, and The Three Sisters are three dramatic masterpieces written by Chekhov that use similar formats to explore a common theme. Each is primarily concerned with the way that passing time wears down human aspirations, and each is haunted by the ghosts of the wasted life. The characters are shown struggling futilely with the lesser problems of life: indecisiveness, loyalty to the wrong cause, and the inability to be clear. These struggles create a mood of sweet, almost aching, sadness that has become known as Chekhovian.
   C. Chekhov's dramatic masterpieces are, along with The Cherry Orchard, Uncle Vanya, and The Three Sisters. These plays share certain thematic and formal similarities. They are concerned most of all with the passage of time and the way in which time erodes human aspirations. Each play is haunted by the specter of the wasted life. Chekhov's characters are caught, however, by life's lesser snares: indecisiveness, loyalty to the wrong cause, and unclarity. The characteristic mood is a sweet, almost aching type of sadness that has come to be known as Chekhovian.
   D. A Chekhovian mood is characterized by sweet, almost aching, sadness. The term comes from three dramatic tragedies by Chekhov which revolve around the sadness of a wasted life. The three masterpieces (Uncle Vanya, The Three Sisters, and The Cherry Orchard) share the same

theme and format. The plays are concerned with how the passage of time erodes human aspirations. They are peopled with characters who are struggling with life's lesser problems. These are people who are indecisive, loyal to the wrong causes, or are unable to make themselves clear.

3.
I. Movie previews have often helped producers decide which parts of movies they should take out or leave in.
II. The first 1933 preview of King Kong was very helpful to the producers because many people ran screaming from the theater and would not return when four men first attacked by Kong were eaten by giant spiders.
III. The 1950 premiere of Sunset Boulevard resulted in the filming of an entirely new beginning, and a delay of six months in the film's release.
IV. In the original opening scene, William Holden was in a morgue talking with thirty-six other "corpses" about the ways some of them had died.
V. When he began to tell them of his life with Gloria Swanson, the audience found this hilarious, instead of taking the scene seriously.

3.____

A. Movie previews have often helped producers decide what parts of movies they should leave in or take out. For example, the first preview of King Kong in 1933 was very helpful. In one scene, four men were first attacked by Kong and then eaten by giant spiders. Many members of the audience ran screaming from the theater and would not return. The premiere of the 1950 film Sunset Boulevard was also very helpful. In the original opening scene, William Holden was in a morgue with thirty-six other "corpses," discussing the ways some of them had died. When he began to tell them of his life with Gloria Swanson, the audience found this hilarious. They were supposed to take the scene seriously. The result was a delay of six months in the release of the film while a new beginning was added.

B. Movie previews have often helped producers decide whether they should change various parts of a movie. After the 1933 preview of King Kong, a scene in which four men who had been attacked by Kong were eaten by giant spiders was taken out as many people ran screaming from the theater and would not return. The 1950 premiere of Sunset Boulevard also led to some changes. In the original opening scene, William Holden was in a morgue talking with thirty-six other "corpses" about the ways some of them had died. When he began to tell them of his life with Gloria Swanson, the audience found this hilarious, instead of taking the scene seriously.

C. What do Sunset Boulevard and King Kong have in common? Both show the value of using movie previews to test audience reaction. The first 1933 preview of King Kong showed that a scene showing four men being eaten by giant spiders after having been attacked by Kong was too frightening for many people. They ran screaming from the theater and couldn't be coaxed back. The 1950 premiere of Sunset Boulevard was also a scream, but not the kind the producers intended. The movie opens with William Holden lying in a morgue discussing the ways they had died with thirty-six other "corpses." When he began to tell them of his life with Gloria Swanson, the audience couldn't take him seriously. Their laughter caused a six-month delay while the beginning was rewritten.

D. Producers very often use movie previews to decide if changes are needed. The premiere of Sunset Boulevard in 1950 led to a new beginning and a six-month delay in film release. At the beginning, William Holden and thirty-six other "corpses" discuss the ways some of them died. Rather than taking this seriously, the audience thought it was hilarious when he began to tell them of his life with Gloria Swanson. The first 1933 preview of King Kong was very helpful for its producers because one scene so terrified the audience that many of them ran screaming from the theater and would not return. In this particular scene, four men who had first been attacked by Kong were eaten by giant spiders.

4.
I. It is common for supervisors to view employees as "things" to be manipulated.
II. This approach does not motivate employees, nor does the carrot-and-stick approach because employees often recognize these behaviors and resent them.
III. Supervisors can change these behaviors by using self-inquiry and persistence.
IV. The best managers genuinely respect those they work with, are supportive and helpful, and are interested in working as a team with those they supervise.
V. They disagree with the Golden Rule that says "he or she who has the gold makes the rules."

4.____

A. Some managers act as if they think the Golden Rule means "he or she who has the gold makes the rules." They show disrespect to employees by seeing them as "things" to be manipulated. Obviously, this approach does not motivate employees any more than the carrot-and-stick approach motivates them. The employees are smart enough to spot these behaviors and resent them. On the other hand, the managers genuinely respect those they work with, are supportive and helpful, and are interested in working as a team. Self-inquiry and persistence can change even the former type of supervisor into the latter.

B. Many supervisors all into the trap of viewing employees as "things" to be manipulated, or try to motivate them by using a carrot-and-stick approach. These methods do not motivate employees, who often recognize the behaviors and resent them. Supervisors can change these behaviors, however, by using self-inquiry and persistence. The best managers are supportive and helpful, and have genuine respect for those with whom they work. They are interested in working as a team with those they supervise. To them, the Golden Rule is not "he or she who has the gold makes the rules."

C. Some supervisors see employees as "things" to be used or manipulated using a carrot-and-stick technique. These methods don't work. Employees often see through them and resent them. A supervisor who wants to change may do so. The techniques of self-inquiry and persistence can be used to turn him or her into the type of supervisor who doesn't think the Golden Rule is "he or she who has the gold makes the rules." They may become like the best managers who treat those with whom they work with respect and give them help and support. These are the manager who know how to build a team.

D. Unfortunately, many supervisors act as if their employees are objects whose movements they can position at will. This mistaken belief has the same result as another popular motivational technique—the carrot-and-stick approach. Both attitudes can lead to the same result—resentment from those employees who recognize the behaviors for what they are. Supervisors who recognize these behaviors can change through the use of persistence and the use of self-inquiry. It's important to remember that the best managers respect their employees. They readily give necessary help and support and are interested in working as a team with those they supervise. To these managers, the Golden Rule is not "he or she who has the gold makes the rules."

5.
I. The first half of the nineteenth century produced a group of pessimistic poets—Byron, De Musset, Heine, Pushkin, and Leopardi.
II. It also produced a group of pessimistic composers—Schubert, Chopin, Schumann, and even the later Beethoven.
III. Above all, in philosophy, there was the profoundly pessimistic philosopher, Schopenhauer.
IV. The Revolution was dead, the Bourbons were restored, the feudal barons were reclaiming their land, and progress everywhere was being suppressed, as the great age was over.
V. "I thank God," said Goethe, "that I am not young in so thoroughly finished a world."

   A. "I thank God," said Goethe, "that I am not young in so thoroughly finished a world." The Revolution was dead, the Bourbons were restored, the feudal barons were reclaiming their land, and progress everywhere was being suppressed. The first half of the nineteenth century produced a group of pessimistic poets: Byron, De Musset, Heine, Pushkin, and Leopardi. It also produced pessimistic composers: Schubert, Chopin, Schumann. Although Beethoven came later, he fits into this group, too. Finally and above all, it also produced a profoundly pessimistic philosopher, Schopenhauer. The great age was over.

   B. The first half of the nineteenth century produced a group of pessimistic poets: Byron, De Musset, Heine, Pushkin, and Leopardi. It produced a group of pessimistic composers: Schubert, Chopin, Schumann, and even the later Beethoven. Above all, it produced a profoundly pessimistic philosopher, Schopenhauer. For each of these men, the great age was over. The Revolution was dead, and the Bourbons were restored. The feudal barons were reclaiming their land, and progress everywhere was being suppressed.

5.____

C. The great age was over. The Revolution was dead—the Bourbons were restored, and the feudal barons were reclaiming their land. Progress everywhere was being suppressed. Out of this climate came a profound pessimism. Poets, like Byron, De Musset, Heine, Pushkin, and Leopardi; composers, like Schubert, Chopin, Schumann, and even the later Beethoven; and above all, a profoundly pessimistic philosopher, Schopenauer. This pessimism which arose in the first half of the nineteenth century is illustrated by these words of Goethe, "I thank God that I am not young in so thoroughly finished a world."

D. The first half of the nineteenth century produced a group of pessimistic poets, Byron, De Musset, Heine, Pushkin, and Leopardi—and a group of pessimistic composers, Schubert, Chopin, Schumann, and the later Beethoven. Above it all, it produced a profoundly pessimistic philosopher, Schopenhauer. The great age was over. The Revolution was dead, the Bourbons were restored, the feudal barons were reclaiming their land, and progress everywhere was being suppressed. "I thank God," said Goethe, "that I am not young in so thoroughly finished a world."

6. I. A new manager sometimes may feel insecure about his or her competence in the new position.
    II. The new manager may then exhibit defensive or arrogant behavior towards those one supervises, or the new manager may direct overly flattering behavior toward one's new supervisor.

    A. Sometimes, a new manager may feel insecure about his or her ability to perform well in this new position. The insecurity may lead him or her to treat others differently. He or she may display arrogant or defensive behavior towards those he or she supervises, or be overly flattering to his or her new supervisor.
    B. A new manager may sometimes feel insecure about his or her ability to perform well in the new position. He or she may then become arrogant, defensive, or overly flattering towards those he or she works with.
    C. There are times when a new manager may be insecure about how well he or she can perform in the new job. The new manager may also behave defensive or act in an arrogant way towards those he or she supervises, or overly flatter his or her boss.
    D. Sometimes a new manager may feel insecure about his or her ability to perform well in the new position. He or she may then display arrogant or defensive behavior towards those they supervise, or become overly flattering towards their supervisors.

6.____

7. I. It is possible to eliminate unwanted behavior by bringing it under stimulus control—tying the behavior to a cue, and then never, or rarely, giving the cue.
    II. One trainer successfully used this method to keep an energetic young porpoise from coming out of her tank whenever she felt like it, which was potentially dangerous.
    III. Her trainer taught her to do it for a reward, in response to a hand signal, and then rarely gave the signal.

7.____

A. Unwanted behavior can be eliminated by tying the behavior to a cue, and then never, or rarely, giving the cue. This is called stimulus control. One trainer was able to use this method to keep an energetic young porpoise from coming out of her tank by teaching her to come out for a reward in response to a hand signal, and then rarely giving the signal.
B. Stimulus control can be used to eliminate unwanted behavior. In this method, behavior is tied to a cue, and then the cue is rarely, if ever, given. One trainer was able to successfully use stimulus control to keep an energetic young porpoise from coming out of her tank whenever she felt like it—a potentially dangerous practice. She taught the porpoise to come out for a reward when she gave a hand signal, and then rarely gave the signal.
C. It is possible to eliminate behavior that is undesirable by bringing it under stimulus control by tying behavior to a signal, and then rarely giving the signal. One trainer successfully used this method to keep an energetic porpoise from coming out of her tank, a potentially dangerous situation. Her trainer taught the porpoise to do it for a reward, in response to a hand signal, and then would rarely give the signal.
D. By using stimulus control, it is possible to eliminate unwanted behavior by tying the behavior to a cue, and then rarely or never give the cue. One trainer was able to use this method to successfully stop a young porpoise from coming out of her tank whenever she felt like it. To curb this potentially dangerous practice, the porpoise was taught by the trainer to come out of the tank for a reward, in response to a hand signal, and then rarely given the signal.

8. I. There is a great deal of concern over the safety of commercial trucks, caused by their greatly increased role in serious accidents since federal deregulation in 1981.
   II. Recently, 60 percent of trucks in New York and Connecticut and 70 percent of trucks in Maryland randomly stopped by state troopers failed safety inspections.
   III. Sixteen states in the United States require no training at all for truck drivers.

   A. Since federal deregulation in 1981, there has been a great deal of concern over the safety of commercial trucks, and their greatly increased role in serious accidents. Recently, 60 percent of trucks in New York and Connecticut, and 70 percent of trucks in Maryland failed safety inspections. Sixteen states in the United States require no training at all for truck drivers.
   B. There is a great deal of concern over the safety of commercial trucks since federal deregulation in 1981. Their role in serious accidents has greatly increased. Recently, 60 percent of trucks randomly stopped in Connecticut and New York and 70 percent in Maryland failed safety inspections conducted by state troopers. Sixteen states in the United States provide no training at all for truck drivers.
   C. Commercial trucks have a greatly increased role in serious accidents since federal deregulation in 1981. This has led to a great deal of concern.

8.____

Recently, 70 percent of trucks in Maryland and 60 percent of trucks in New York and Connecticut failed inspection of those that were randomly stopped by state troopers. Sixteen states in the United States require no training for all truck drivers.

D. Since federal deregulation in 1981, the role that commercial trucks have played in serious accidents has greatly increased, and this has led to a great deal of concern. Recently, 60 percent of trucks in New York and Connecticut, and 70 percent of trucks in Maryland randomly stopped by state troopers failed safety inspections. Sixteen states in the U.S. don't require any training for truck drivers.

9.
I. No matter how much some people have, they still feel unsatisfied and want more, or want to keep what they have forever.
II. One recent television documentary showed several people flying from New York to Paris for a one-day shopping spree to buy platinum earrings, because they were bored.
III. In Brazil, some people were ordering coffins that cost a minimum of $45,000 and are equipping them with deluxe stereos, televisions, and other graveyard necessities.

A. Some people, despite having a great deal, still feel unsatisfied and want more, or think they can keep what they have forever. One recent documentary on television showed several people enroute from Paris to New York for a one day shopping spree to buy platinum earrings, because they were bored. Some people in Brazil are even ordering coffins equipped with such graveyard necessities as deluxe stereos and televisions. The price of the coffins start at $45,000.
B. No matter how much some people have, they may feel unsatisfied. This leads them to want more, or to want to keep what they have forever. Recently, a television documentary depicting several people flying from New York to Paris for a one day shopping spree to buy platinum earrings. They were bored. Some people in Brazil are ordering coffins that cost at least $45,000 and come equipped with deluxe televisions, stereos and other necessary graveyard items.
C. Some people will be dissatisfied no matter how much they have. They may want more, or they may want to keep what they have forever. One recent television documentary showed several people, motivated by boredom, jetting from New York to Paris for a one-day shopping spree to buy platinum earrings. In Brazil, some people are ordering coffins equipped with deluxe stereos, televisions and other graveyard necessities. The minimum price for these coffins—$45,000.
D. Some people are never satisfied. No matter how much they have they still want more, or think they can keep what they have forever. One television documentary recently showed several people flying from New York to Paris for the day to buy platinum earrings because they were bored. In Brazil, some people are ordering coffins that cost $45,000 and are equipped with deluxe stereos, televisions and other graveyard necessities.

9._____

10.
    I. A television signal or video signal has three parts.

    II. Its parts are the black-and-white portion, the color portion, and the synchronizing (sync) pulses, which keep the picture stable.

    III. Each video source, whether it's a camera or a video-cassette recorder contains its own generator of these synchronizing pulses to accompany the picture that it's sending in order to keep it steady and straight.

    IV. In order to produce a clean recording, a video-cassette recorder must "lock-up" to the sync pulses that are part of the video it is trying to record, and this effort may be very noticeable if the device does not have gunlock.

10.____

    A. There are three parts to a television or video signal: the black-and-white part, the color part, and the synchronizing (sync) pulses, which keep the picture stable. Whether it's a video-cassette recorder or a camera, each video source contains its own pulse that synchronizes and generates the picture it's sending in order to keep it straight and steady. A video-cassette recorder must "lock up" to the sync pulses that are part of the video it's trying to record. If the device doesn't have gunlock, this effort must be very noticeable.

    B. A video signal or television is comprised of three parts: the black-and-white portion, the color portion, and the sync (synchronizing) pulses, which keep the picture stable. Whether it's a camera or a video-cassette recorder, each video source contains its own generator of these synchronizing pulses. These accompany the picture that it's sending in order to keep it straight and steady. A video-cassette recorder must "lock up" to the sync pulses that are part of the video it is trying to record in order to produce a clean recording. This effort may be very noticeable if the device does not have gunlock.

    C. There are three parts to a television or video signal: the color portion, the black-and-white portion, and the sync (synchronizing pulses). These keep the picture stable. Each video source, whether it's a video-cassette recorder or a camera, generates these synchronizing pulses accompanying the picture it's sending in order to keep it straight and steady. If a clean recording is to be produced, a video-cassette recorder must store the sync pulses that are part of the video it is trying to record. This effort may not be noticeable if the device does not have gunlock.

    D. A television signal or video signal has three parts: the black-and-white portion, the color portion, and the synchronizing (sync) pulses. It's the sync pulses which keep the picture stable, which accompany it and keep it steady and straight. Whether it's a camera or a video-cassette recorder, each video source contains its own generator of these synchronizing pulses. To produce a clean recording, a video-cassette recorder must "lock up" to the sync pulses that are part of the video it is trying to record. If the device does not have gunlock, this effort may be very noticeable.

KEY (CORRECT ANSWERS)

1. C
2. B
3. A
4. B
5. D

6. A
7. B
8. D
9. C
10. D

EXAMINATION SECTION

TEST 1

DIRECTIONS: Each question or incomplete statement is followed by several suggested answers or completions. Select the one that BEST answers the question or completes the statement. *PRINT THE LETTER OF THE CORRECT ANSWER IN THE SPACE AT THE RIGHT.*

Questions 1-4.

DIRECTIONS: Questions 1 through 4 are to be answered on the basis of the following passage.

A State department which is interested in finding acceptable solutions to the operational problems of specific types of community self-help organizations recently sent two of its staff members to meet with one such organization. At that meeting, the leaders of the community organization voiced the need for increased activity planning input of a more detailed nature from the citizens regularly served by that organization. There followed a discussion of a number of information-gathering methods, including surveys by telephone, questionnaires mailed to the citizens' residences, in-person interviews with the citizens, and the placing of suggestion boxes in the organization's headquarters building. Concern was expressed by one of the leaders that the organization's funds be spent judiciously. The State department representatives present promised to investigate the possibility of a matching fund grant of money to the organization.

Later, the proposed survey was conducted using questionnaires completed by those citizens who visited the organization's headquarters. The results of the survey included the information that twice as many citizens wanted more educational activities scheduled than wanted more social activities scheduled, whereas one-half of those who wanted more educational activities scheduled were interested mainly in special job training.

1. A similar survey conducted by a State department employee involved special job training. That survey uncovered the information below. The following four sentences are to be rearranged to form the most effective and logical paragraph.
   Select the letter representing the BEST sequence for these sentences.
   I. The majority of those who are still in this group are ethnic minorities.
   II. The number of economically disadvantaged people who enjoyed their special job training is larger than the number of economically disadvantaged people who did not enjoy it.
   III. Thirty-five percent of all those who are economically disadvantaged are not ethnic minorities.
   IV. Eighty percent of those who have completed special job training in the past ten years are economically disadvantaged.
   The CORRECT answer is:
   A. IV, I, III, II   B. I, III, II, IV   C. IV, II, I, III   D. I, II, III, IV

1.____

2. In the above reading passage, the word *judiciously* means MOST NEARLY
   A. legally   B. immediately   C. prudently   D. uniformly

2.____

3. Based only on the information in the reading passage, which one of the following statements is MOST fully supported?
   A. The leaders of the community organization in question wanted to increase the quantity and quality of feedback about that organization's suggestion boxes.
   B. The number of citizens surveyed who wanted more educational activities scheduled and were mainly interested in special job training was the same as the number of citizens surveyed who wanted more social activities to be scheduled.
   C. At the meeting concerned, matching funds were promised to the community organization in question by the two State department representatives present.
   D. Telephone surveys generally yield more accurate information than do surveys conducted through the use of mailed questionnaires.

3.____

4. The following four sentences are to be rearranged to form the most effective and logical paragraph.
   Select the letter representing the BEST sequence for these sentences.
   I. Formal surveys of citizens within a community also convey to those citizens the interest of the community leadership in hearing the citizens' ideas about community improvement.
   II. Such surveys can provide needed input into the process of establishing specific community program goals.
   III. Formally conducted surveys of community residents often yield valuable information to the local area leaders responsible for community-based programs.
   IV. No community should formulate these goals without attempting to obtain the views of its citizenry.
   The CORRECT answer is:
   A. III, I, IV, II   B. I, III, II, IV   C. III, II, IV, I   D. IV, III, II, I

4.____

Questions 5-8.

DIRECTIONS: Questions 5 through 8 are to be answered on the basis of the following passage.

The Smith Paint Company, which currently employs 2,000 persons, has been in existence for 20 years. A new chemical plant, Futuron, was recently developed by an employee of that company. This paint was released for public use a month ago on a trial basis. The sales were phenomenal, and there is a great demand for more Futuron to be manufactured. The profits to be made by increased manufacturing and sale of Futuron could place the Smith Paint Company in a leading role in the paint industry.

The Smith Paint Company currently produces 2 million gallons of the more traditional paint per year. The Smith Paint Company's Board of Directors wishes to reduce its production of this traditional paint by 50%, and to produce 1 million gallons of Futuron per year.

The employees are quite concerned about this potential production change. A public nonprofit research group has been investigating the chemical make-up of Futuron. Initial research indicates that negative physical reactions may result from working closely with the chemicals necessary to manufacture Futuron. For this reason, most of the company employees do not want the proposed change in production to occur. The members of the Board of Directors, however, argue that the research results are too inconclusive to cause great concern. They say that the company would lose 25% to 50% of its potential profit if the large-scale manufacturing of Futuron is not initiated immediately.

5. Seventy-five percent of the Smith Paint Company's current employees were hired during its first 10 years of operation. Fifteen percent were hired in the past five years. During the five-year interval between the first ten years and the most recent five years, 40 persons were hired per year.
   What percentage of its total employees were hired during the Smith Paint Company's first 13 years of operation?
   A. 75%   B. 81%   C. 85%   D. 90%

6. Assume that the total possible profit the Smith Paint Company could make during its first year of manufacturing the proposed amount of Futuron would be $1.00 per gallon. The purchase of new machinery would reduce this first-year profit by 50%. The anticipated delay, during the first production year, in establishing large-scale manufacturing facilities would reduce the total possible profit by an additional 25%.
   Given this information, what would be the actual profit made from the first year of manufacturing Futuron?
   A. $250,000   B. $375,000   C. $500,000   D. $750,000

7. In the reading passage, the word *inconclusive* means MOST NEARLY
   A. ineluctable   B. incorrect
   C. unreasonable   D. indeterminate

8. Based on the information in the reading passage, which of the following statements represents the MOST accurate conclusion?
   A. The proposed reduction in the production of its traditional paint would not financially injure the Smith Paint Company.
   B. A greater proportion of the Smith Paint Company's employees are in favor of the proposed increase in Futuron production than are opposed to it.
   C. The increased Futuron production proposed by the Smith Paint Company's Board of Directors would cause that company's employees considerable health damage.
   D. Positive public response to the sale of Futuron suggests that considerable profit can be made by increasing the manufacturing and sale of Futuron.

KEY (CORRECT ANSWERS)

1. A
2. C
3. B
4. C
5. B
6. A
7. D
8. D

SOLUTIONS TO PROBLEMS

1. For the following reasons, Choice A is correct and the other three choices are incorrect.

    a. Both Choice B and Choice D begin with Sentence I, which states, *The majority of those who are still in this group are ethnic minorities.* The paragraph cannot logically begin with a statement such as Sentence I, because no one reading the paragraph would know what *this group* refers to. Therefore, Choice B and Choice D are not correct and may be eliminated from consideration.

    b. Both Choice A and Choice B begin with Sentence IV, which states, *Eighty percent of those who have completed special job training in the past ten years are economically disadvantaged.* The problem then becomes selecting the best sequence of the other three sentences so that they most logically follow the initial Sentence IV.

    c. If you select Choice C, then you are choosing Sentence II as the correct second sentence. Sentence II states, *The number of economically disadvantaged people who enjoyed their special job training is larger than the number of economically disadvantaged people who did not enjoy it.* Then Sentence I would be the third sentence. However, that would not be logical, because you could not tell whether *this group* in Sentence I refers to *economically disadvantaged people who enjoyed their special job training* or whether *this group* refers to *economically people who did not enjoy it.* Therefore, Choice C is not correct.

    d. By the process of elimination, only Choice A remains. Choice A specifies Sentence I as the second sentence, which is logically correct in that *this group* in Sentence I will then refer to those who are *economically disadvantaged* in Sentence IV. The two remaining sentences also refer back to *economically disadvantaged*, thus creating a paragraph that reads logically from start to finish. Therefore, Choice A is the correct answer.

2. Choices B and D should be eliminated from further consideration due to the context in which the word *judiciously* was used in the reading passage. Specifically, concern was expressed that funds be spent judiciously. Nothing in the paragraph suggests a need for concern if the funds were not spent immediately or uniformly. Choice A must be considered, because public funds should be spent legally. However, the word *judiciously* is related to the word *judgment* rather than to the word *judiciary*. It is the latter word that has to do with courts of law and is related to legality, so Choice A is incorrect. On the other hand, *judiciously* and *prudently* both mean *wisely* and *with direction*. Therefore, Choice C is correct.

3. Choice B is the correct choice. No matter what numbers you apply, Choice B still will be correct. This is because when you multiply any number by two and then divide the result in half, you end up with the same number that you begin with. For example, suppose that 20 citizens wanted more social activities. Twice that number (40 citizens) wanted more educational activities. But of those 40 citizens, one-half (20 citizens) wanted mainly special job training.

Choice A is incorrect because, first of all, the organization did not have any suggestion boxes; although suggestion boxes were discussed, questionnaires ultimately were used instead. In addition, Choice A is incorrect because it was input about the planning of activities that the leaders of the community organization wanted rather than feedback concerning suggestion boxes.

Choice C also is not correct. Instead of promising the matching funds, the State department representatives promised to investigate (or look into) the possibility of obtaining the matching funds.

Choice D is incorrect because the reading passage does not tell whether telephone surveys or mailed questionnaires provide more accurate information. Remember, the instructions for this question state that the question is to be answered ONLY on the information in the applicable reading passage.

4. The correct answer is Choice C. Choice A and Choice C both begin with Sentence III, which certainly could be the logical first sentence of a paragraph. However, the next sentence (Sentence I) in Choice A leaves the initial topic of obtaining information from citizens. The third sentence in Choice A would be Sentence IV, *No community should formulate these goals without attempting to obtain the views of its citizenry*. The words *these goals* do not logically refer to anything in the previous two sentences, so Choice A is incorrect.

Choice B also is incorrect because the word *also* in its first sentence (Sentence I) has nothing to logically refer to. *Also* would have to be used in a sentence that comes later in the paragraph.

Choice D has the same problem as Choice A. Choice D begins with Sentence IV, which starts off, *No community should formulate these goals....* Again, the words *these goals* need to refer to something in a previous sentence about goals in order to be logically correct.

5. Choice B is correct. Here are the mathematical computations you might use to arrive at the correct answer of 81%.

   a. The reading passage states that the Smith Paint Company currently employs 2,000 persons. The first part of this question states that 75% of those current employees were hired during the first ten years that the company was in operation. By multiplying 75% by 2,000, you would find that 1,500 of the current employees were hired during the company's first ten years.

   b. The question asks about the first 13 years of the company's operation rather than just the first ten years. Therefore, you need the arithmetical information for the three years that immediately followed the first ten years. You know from the reading passage that the company has been operating for 20 years. You have the information for the first ten years. Twenty minus ten leaves the most recent ten years.

c. You know from the question that 40 persons were hired each year during the five-year period of time between the first ten years and the most recent five years. However, you need the information about only the first three years. By multiplying 40 persons per year by three years, you would find that 120 people were hired during the first three years that came immediately after the first ten years of the company's operation.

d. Next, you would need to add 1,500 people (for the first ten years) and 120 people (for the next three years). That would give you a total of 1,620 people hired during the first 13 years.

e. The question asks for the percentage of the Smith Paint Company's total employees hired during its first 13 years. You know that the total number of employees is 2,000. The question then is: 1,620 people is what percentage of 2,000 people? By dividing 2,000 into 1,620, you would find that the correct answer is 81%.

Choice A is incorrect because it deals with only the first ten years that the company was in operation, rather than the first 13 years. If you took 1,500 people (from Step a in the explanatory material for the correct answer) and divided that number by 2,000 people, you would arrive at 75%, which is not correct.

Choice C is incorrect. If you correctly arrived at 1,500 people for the first ten years but then incorrectly dealt with the next five years instead of the next three years, you would end up with the wrong answer of 85%. First, you would multiply 40 people by five years and end up with 200 people. Next, you would add 200 to 1,500 and end up with 1,700 people. Finally, you would divide 1,700 by 2,000 and get 85%.

Choice D also is incorrect. If you correctly arrived at 1,500 people for the first ten years but then used the information for the most recent five years instead of the information for the five years that came just before the most recent five years, you would end up with the incorrect answer of 90%. First, you would find from the question that 15% of the total employees were hired in the past five years. Next, you would multiply 15% by 2,000 total employees and end up with 300. Next, you would add 1,500 employees and 300 employees, ending up with a total of 1,800 employees. By dividing 1,800 by 2,000, you would arrive at 90%.

6. Choice A is correct. Here are the mathematical computations you would need to make to arrive at the correct answer of $250,000.

a. The reading passage states that the amount of Futuron proposed for manufacture each year is 1 million gallons. The question states that the possible profit per gallon would be $1.00. By multiplying $1.00 by 1,000,000, you would find that $1,000,000 would be the total possible profit to be made during the first year.

b. The question states that the $1,000,000 possible profit would have to be reduced by 50% because of the purchase of new machinery, plus by an additional 25% due to the delay in establishing manufacturing facilities. The possible profit must, therefore, be reduced by 50% plus 25%, or by a total of 75%, leaving only 25% of the $1,000,000 as possible profit.

c. By multiplying 25% by $1,000,000, you would arrive at $250,000 as the actual profit which would be made.

Choice B is incorrect. If the two profit reductions were incorrectly multiplied by one another (50% times 25%) and the product (12½%) added to 50%, there would have been a net reduction of 62 ½%, yielding $375,000. However, the two profit reductions are independent of each other and should be added together.

Choice C also is incorrect. It would occur if you only took into account the 50% profit reduction. However, as the paragraph states, you must also deduct an additional 25% of the total profit.

Choice D ($75,000) would be made if you incorrectly multiplied the total profit reduction (75%) by $1,000,000. However, the question asks for the profit, not the profit reduction.

7. Both *indeterminate* and *inconclusive* mean *vague* and *indefinite*, so Choice D is correct. Choice A is incorrect, because the word *ineluctable* means *inescapable* or *inevitable*. The reading passage does not support the conclusion that the research results are incorrect or unreasonable, so Choice B and Choice C can be eliminated from consideration.

8. Choice D is correct. The reading passage states, *The sales were phenomenal, and there is a great demand for more Futuron to be manufactured. The profits to be made by increasing the manufacturing and sale of Futuron could place the Smith Paint Company in a leading role in the paint industry.* Since the sales of Futuron were phenomenal (remarkable; extraordinary) and there still is a great demand for it, the suggestion of considerable future profit is reasonable.

Choice A is not the most accurate conclusion based on the reading passage. The financial impact of decreasing the production of the traditional paint cannot be ascertained. Therefore, it is not certain that the proposed 50% reduction in the manufacturing of the Smith Paint Company's traditional paint would not financially injure that company. Certainly, Choice D is a more accurate conclusion.

Choice B is incorrect. A greater proportion of the employees being in favor of the proposed increase in Futuron production than not being in favor of it implies that over 50% of the employees are in favor of it. However, the reading passage states that most of the employees (which, logically, means over 50% of the employees) do not want the proposed change to occur.

Choice C also is not the most accurate conclusion. It states that the proposed increase in Futuron production would cause employees considerable health damage. The reading passage is not definite on this issue of health damage. It states, *Initial research indicates that negative physical reactions may result from working closely with the chemicals necessary....* How serious the health damage might be is not stated in the reading passage.

PREPARING WRITTEN MATERIALS

EXAMINATION SECTION
TEST 1

DIRECTIONS: Each of the two sentences in the following questions may contain errors in punctuation, capitalization, or grammar.
If there is an error in only Sentence I, mark your answer A. If there is an error in only Sentence II, mark your answer B.
If there is an error in both Sentence I and Sentence II, mark your answer C. If both Sentence I and II are correct, mark your answer D.
PRINT THE LETTER OF THE CORRECT ANSWER IN THE SPACE AT THE RIGHT.

1. I. The task of typing these reports is to be divided equally between you and me. 1.____
   II. If it was he, I would use a different method for filing these records.

2. I. The new clerk is just as capable as some of the older employees, if not more capable. 2.____
   II. Using his knowledge of arithmetic to check the calculation, the supervisor found no errors in the report.

3. I. A typist who does consistently superior work probably merits promotion. 3.____
   II. In its report on the stenographic unit, the committee pointed out that neither the stenographers nor the typists were adequately trained.

4. I. Entering the office, the desk was noticed immediately by the visitor. 4.____
   II. Arrangements have been made to give this training to whoever applies for it.

5. I. The office manager estimates that this assignment, which is to be handled by you and I, will require about two weeks for completion. 5.____
   II. One of the recommendations of the report is that these kind of forms be discarded because they are of no value.

6. I. The supervisor knew that the typist was a quiet, cooperative, efficient, employee. 6.____
   II. The duties of stenographer are to take dictation notes at conferences and transcribing them.

7. I. The stenographer has learned that she, as well as two typists, is being assigned to the new unit. 7.____
   II. We do not know who you have designated to take charge of the new program.

8. I. He asked, "When do you expect to return?" 8.____
   II. I doubt whether this system will be successful here; it is not suitable for the work of our agency.

9. I. It is a policy of this agency to encourage punctuality as a good habit for we employees to adopt.
   II. The successful completion of the task was due largely to them cooperating effectively with the supervisor.

10. I. Mr. Smith, who is a very competent executive has offered his services to our department.
    II. Every one of the stenographers who work in this office is considered trustworthy.

11. I. It is very annoying to have a pencil sharpener, which is not in proper working order.
    II. The building watchman checked the door of Charlie's office and found that the lock has been jammed.

12. I. Since he went on the New York City council a year ago, one of his primary concerns has been safety in the streets.
    II. After waiting in the doorway for about 15 minutes, a black sedan appeared.

13. I. When you are studying a good textbook is important.
    II. He said he would divide the money equally between you and me.

14. I. The question is, "How can a large number of envelopes be sealed rapidly without the use of sealing machine?"
    II. The administrator assigned two stenographers, Mary and I, to the new bureau.

15. I. A dictionary, in addition to the office management textbooks, were placed on his desk.
    II. The concensus of opinion is that none of the employees should be required to work overtime.

16. I. Mr. Granger has demonstrated that he is as courageous, if not more courageous, than Mr. Brown.
    II. The successful completion of the project depends on the manager's accepting our advisory opinion.

17. I. Mr. Ames was in favor of issuing a set of rules and regulations for all of us employees to follow.
    II. It is inconceivable that the new clerk knows how to deal with that kind of correspondence.

18. I. The revised referrence manual is to be used by all of the employees.
    II. Mr. Johnson told Miss Kent and me to accumulate all the letters that we receive.

19. I. The supervisor said, that before any changes would be made in the attendance report, there must be ample justification for them.
    II. Each of them was asked to amend their preliminary report.

20. I. Mrs. Peters conferred with Mr. Roberts before she laid the papers on his desk.
    II. As far as this report is concerned, Mr. Williams always has and will be responsible for its preparation.

20.____

KEY (CORRECT ANSWERS)

1.	B	11.	C
2.	D	12.	C
3.	D	13.	A
4.	A	14.	B
5.	C	15.	C
6.	C	16.	A
7.	B	17.	B
8.	D	18.	A
9.	C	19.	C
10.	A	20.	B

TEST 2

DIRECTIONS: Each question or incomplete statement is followed by several suggested answers or completions. Select the one that BEST answers the question or completes the statement. *PRINT THE LETTER OF THE CORRECT ANSWER IN THE SPACE AT THE RIGHT.*

Questions 1-9.

DIRECTIONS: Questions 1 through 9 consist of pairs of sentences which may or may not contain errors in grammar, capitalization, or punctuation.
If both sentences are correct, mark your answer A.
If the first sentence only is correct, mark your answer B.
If the second sentence only is correct, mark your answer C.
If both sentences are incorrect, mark your answer D.
NOTE: Consider a sentence correct if it contains no errors, although there may be other correct ways of writing the sentence.

1. I. An unusual conference will be held today at George Washington high school. 1.____
    II. The principal of the school, Dr. Pace, described the meeting as "a unique opportunity for educators to exchange ideas.

2. I. Studio D, which they would ordinarily use, will be occupied at that time. 2.____
    II. Any other studio, which is properly equipped, may be used instead.

3. I. D.H. Lawrence's <u>Sons and Lovers</u> were discussed on today's program. 3.____
    II. Either Eliot's or Yeats's work is to be covered next week.

4. I. This program is on the air for three years now, and has a well-established audience. 4.____
    II. We have received many complimentary letters from listeners, and scarcely no critical ones.

5. I. Both Mr. Owen and Mr. Mitchell have addressed the group. 5.____
    II. As has Mr. Stone, whose talks have been especially well received.

6. I. The original program was different in several respects from the version that eventually went on the air. 6.____
    II. Each of the three announcers who Mr. Scott thought had had suitable experience was asked whether he would be willing to take on the special assignment.

7. I. A municipal broadcasting system provides extensive coverage of local events, but also reports national and international news. 7.____
    II. A detailed account of happenings in the South may be carried by a local station hundreds of miles away.

8. I. Jack Doe the announcer and I will be working on the program. 8.____
    II. The choice of musical selections has been left up to he and I.

140

9. I. Mr. Taylor assured us that "he did not anticipate any difficulty in making arrangements for the broadcast."
    II. Although there had seemed at first to be certain problems; these had been solved.

Questions 10-14.

DIRECTIONS: Questions 10 through 14 consist of pairs of sentences which may contain errors in grammar, sentence structure, punctuation, or spelling, or both sentences may be correct. Consider a sentence correct if it contains no errors, although there may be other correct ways of writing the sentence.
If only Sentence I contains an error, mark your answer A.
If only Sentence II contains an error, mark your answer B.
If both sentences contain errors, mark your answer C.
If both sentences are correct, mark your answer D.

10. I. No employee considered to be indispensable will be assigned to the new office.
    II. The arrangement of the desks and chairs give the office a neat appearance.

11. I. The recommendation, accompanied by a report, was delivered this morning.
    II. Mr. Green thought the procedure would facilitate his work; he knows better now.

12. I. Limiting the term "property" to tangible property, in the criminal mischief setting, accords with prior case law holding that only tangible property came within the purview of the offense of malicious mischief.
    II. Thus, a person who intentionally destroys the property of another, but under an honest belief that he has title to such property, cannot be convicted of criminal mischief under the Revised Penal Law.

13. I. Very early in its history, New York enacted statutes from time to time punishing, either as a felony or as a misdemeanor, malicious injuries to various kinds of property: piers, booms, dams, bridges, etc.
    II. The application of the statute is necessarily restricted to trespassory takings with larcenous intent: namely with intent permanently or virtually permanently to "appropriate" property or "deprive" the owner of its use.

14. I. Since the former Penal Law did not define the instruments of forgery in a general fashion, its crime of forgery was held to be narrower than the common law offense in this respect and to embrace only those instruments explicitly specified in the substantive provisions.
    II. After entering the barn through an open door for the purpose of stealing, it was closed by the defendants.

Questions 15-20.

DIRECTIONS: Questions 15 through 20 consist of pairs of sentences which may or may not contain errors in grammar, capitalization, or punctuation.
If both sentences are correct, mark your answer A.
If the first sentence only is correct, mark your answer B.
If the second sentence only is correct, mark your answer C.
If both sentences are incorrect, mark your answer D.
NOTE: Consider a sentence correct if it contains no errors, although there may be other ways of writing the sentence.

15. I. The program, which is currently most popular, is a news broadcast. 15.____
    II. The engineer assured his supervisor that there was no question of his being late again.

16. I. The announcer recommended that the program originally scheduled for that time be cancelled. 16.____
    II. Copies of the script may be given to whoever is interested.

17. I. A few months ago it looked like we would be able to broadcast the concert live. 17.____
    II. The program manager, as well as the announcers, were enthusiastic about the plan.

18. I. No speaker on the subject of education is more interesting than he. 18.____
    II. If he would have had the time, we would have scheduled him for a regular weekly broadcast.

19. I. This quartet, in its increasingly complex variations on a simple theme, admirably illustrates Professor Baker's point. 19.____
    II. Listeners interested in these kind of ideas will find his recently published study of Haydn rewarding.

20. I. The Commissioner's resignation at the end of next month marks the end of a long public service career. 20.____
    II. Outstanding among his numerous achievements were his successful implementation of several revolutionary schemes to reorganize the agency.

KEY (CORRECT ANSWERS)

1.	C	11.	D
2.	B	12.	C
3.	C	13.	B
4.	D	14.	A
5.	B	15.	C
6.	A	16.	A
7.	A	17.	D
8.	D	18.	B
9.	D	19.	B
10.	B	20.	B

www.ingramcontent.com/pod-product-compliance
Lightning Source LLC
Chambersburg PA
CBHW081823300426
44116CB00014B/2465